Where did Jim and Pat discover the awesome power that delivers from depression and fear? How did Valerie, wracked with pain, find the wondrous force that cures the incurable, making her healthy and strong? What gave Denise the inward strength to fall more deeply in love with her unfaithful husband, restoring their marriage? What force reunited Bill with his parents when he seemed to have dropped out of the world? How did each of these people, searching desperately for answers, find a life-changing avenue to peace, health, and happiness?

They asked for and received agape love—the love that takes over where our human love leaves off. And in each of these true situations, a miracle took place!

Agape love succeeds where our love fails!

To Kevin and Doug
who left their boats
to follow Jesus.

The author has written articles for
Cross and Crown, *Spiritual Life*,
*Our Family, Emmanuel, Koinonia,
Renewal Magazine (London),* and
Franciscan Herald.

the miracle of agape LOVE

by JOSEPH F. MANNING

 *Whitaker House*

THE MIRACLE OF AGAPE LOVE

Reverend Joseph Manning
P.O. Box 1077
Bristol, Connecticut 06010

© Copyright by Joseph F. Manning 1977
Printed in the United States of America
ISBN: 0-88368-079-3

Some of the names have been changed to protect the individuals involved. The events are as described.

All Bible quotations are from the *King James Version* except those identified *NASB* which are from *The New American Standard Bible*, © The Lockman Foundation 1960, 1962, 1963, 1968, 1971, 1972, 1973, 1975, used by permission.

CONTENTS

FOREWORD

THE MIRACLE OF AGAPE LOVE is extraordinarily good. I am sure that thousands of persons will be blessed—and transformed—as a result of reading this book. One of its most important contributions is to those caught up in epidemic marital problems. Joseph Manning not only offers a scriptural solution to those problems, but he gives a clear-cut word to those who need to know afresh the love of God.

Pat Robertson, President
Christian Broadcasting Network

PREFACE

What Is Agape Love?

Poets and philosophers down through the centuries have spoken eloquently about the joys and sorrows of human love. Indeed, more poems in the English language have been written about love than any other topic. Few will forget Elizabeth Barrett Browning's classic expression of the depth and breadth of love in the poem entitled, "How Do I Love Thee?" for poetic words have a way of wooing the human heart. Even in today's greeting cards, men and women attempt to capture in a few words of verse the appropriate sentiment of love felt toward a beloved; be it a sweetheart, a wife, a husband or a child.

Yet, who will write a poem about the limitations of love when a cheek no longer flushes with the bloom of youth, or when a furrowed brow is scaly and weatherbeaten from old age? Who will write the verse that tells it like it is when love diminishes because the beloved has betrayed the lover? Finally, who will write the poem about the death of love in a relationship that withers from boredom or monotony?

If we are honest, we will admit that much of our loving is limited. We tend to love only those who return it, and as time progresses we become guarded in love to the degree that each of us has been hurt in it. Even as Christians, we discover that many of our relationships leave something to be desired when it comes to giving love.

There are many lessons that we have to learn in the Christian walk, and very often, the lesson on love is where we seem to constantly fall short. Perhaps it is because loving others is so all-embracing. It touches on almost every aspect of our lives. It involves all of our relationships with people and covers all the commandments.

Misunderstandings about love most often lead to our failures in it. The world has caused us to think of love in a Pollyanna fashion as though it were merely a good feeling that we must have for everyone. And, we tend to see Christian love as something that is manufactured by human hands, something that we should automatically possess. As a result of such misunderstandings, Christians are afraid to admit that they dislike, or have not found the strength to love, a particular person. But, each of us are faced continually with situations that are impossible to cope with in our own strength. We are forced to admit that we find ourselves powerless at times to love certain people, whether they are Christians or not. Discouraged, we usually view these difficulties in love as great failures on our part.

I maintain that there is no substitute for a personal relationship with Jesus Christ. Yet, we must grow and mature in this relationship. As we do grow, we realize that despite our weaknesses, we have access to the throne of grace. Seeing our dislikes for others as something God can change in us, we can learn to take these failures to Jesus and move from defeat in love to victory.

But, just how important to our Christian walk is this victory?

A quick glance at any concordance of the Bible shows us how many times the word *love* appears. This isn't surprising when we remember how important this theme is throughout the Bible. Jesus Himself showed us how the law of love fulfills the law of the Old Testament. Indeed, love is the new law. And since *love* is so strongly emphasized in the New Testament, it should be fully understood in the minds and hearts of all Christians.

Some time ago, I decided to look at the word *love* in the Greek New Testament in order to discover its purest meaning. Following it throughout, I was greatly surprised to discover the word *agape* (pronounced ä gäp′ pā) in its place in almost every instance. Another word for love which appears occasionally is *phileo*. The word *agape* means a godly love, a higher love, while the word *phileo* means brotherly love or affection.

In John 17:23, we begin to realize that *agape* is the love of the Father for the Son as Jesus says to His Father, "for thou *lovedst* me before the foundation of the world." Then, in John 3:16, we see that *agape* is the very love that God has for the human race, "for God so *loved* the world, that he gave his only begotten Son, that whosoever believeth in him shall not perish, but have everlasting life;" and not merely for those who are saved because Romans 5:8 tells us that God loved us with *agape* love while we were yet sinners. God's love carries with it the promise already fulfilled, "I love you enough that I would give My life for you."

As I continued my study, I discovered to my amazement that *agape* is the very same love that God expects of His children! In John 13:34 Jesus revealed to his disciples, "A new commandment I give unto you, that ye love one another; *as I have loved you*, that ye also love one another."

Exactly what, then, is this *agape* love to which we are called?

It is a God-given love that the Lord commands us to

give back to Him as well as to others—a love that no one, in his own strength and by his own effort, could possibly have. *Agape* does not flow from the nature of man; it is, in fact, alien to it. *Agape* love flows from the heart of God, through us, to one another when we yield ourselves as channels.

Agape is God's love to us and God's love *in* us. It is the love that bears all things, believes all things, hopes all things and endures all things.

It is the same kind of love shown by each of the individuals in the following true stories. In nearly every instance, the person in the story asked for and received God's *agape* love—*the love that takes over where our own human love leaves off.* And because of God's *agape* love in each situation, a miracle took place.

God's *agape* love succeeds where our love fails!

AGAPE LOVE

HEALS BROKEN HOMES

I sat listening intently to the nervous male voice on the other end of the telephone. "You don't know me, but someone gave me your name and thought that you could help me with my problem. My name is Bob and my problem is my wife. I'm afraid I'm going to have to commit her to an institution, but I need your help."

"I'll be glad to help you, if I can," I told him. "What do you want me to do?"

Bob's voice dropped almost to a whisper, as though fearful that his next sentence might be overheard. "I think that my wife, Denise, has become a religious fanatic," he said guardedly. "I need the approval of a minister that she needs psychiatric help from an institution. This whole situation is driving me bananas," he added. "Is there any way we can get together today for lunch? I'm afraid to meet you at my house. I don't want Denise to hear us talking about her condition."

I assured Bob that I would meet him at a downtown restaurant for lunch, wondering what was in store for me. I was only spending a few days ministering in this section of Oregon, before returning to New England.

Not knowing the area, I arrived about ten minutes late for our appointment. A man was in front of the restaurant, smoking nervously and pacing like an expectant father. I walked up and greeted him, certain that this was Bob. He was a strapping man, well-dressed and standing six feet, four inches tall. My immediate impression was of an irritated and troubled person. His greeting confirmed my thoughts.

"Thanks for coming, Reverend Manning," Bob said, running his fingers nervously through his hair. "I just can't live with this situation much longer."

We entered the busy restaurant and found a table in the back. Early in the conversation, I discovered that Bob and his wife, Denise, were in their mid-thirties and had four children. I discerned from his clothing and manner of speaking that Bob was a successful businessman.

After we ordered our lunch, Bob said to me, "Don't get me wrong. I'm not a religious man, but I know when things are getting carried away." I asked him if he ever went to church. "I haven't been to church for seven years," he answered, "because of my job." When I asked him if he worked on Sundays, he replied, "No, I'm just too tired to do anything but sleep."

With that our soup arrived, and Bob, who was chain-smoking, said, "This wife of mine is driving me up a wall. Her problems began when she went to this prayer meeting. Church on Sunday morning wasn't enough for her. She had to go to this strange place where they 'speak in tongues.' I think she became what is called a charismatic. She goes around the house saying 'Praise God' all day and all night long."

At that point it was all I could do not to laugh. Little did he know that he was sitting across from another charismatic. Not only did I *understand* his wife's "problem," I *shared* it!

"Denise smiles too much," Bob continued. "She smiles when things are good and she smiles when things are bad.

14

I'm worried 'cause I think she's lost all her marbles! She prays over the fruit and the food. She prays over everyone that comes into the house. And what *really* bugs me is when she prays over me while I'm asleep. That really drives me crazy!" Bob was so keyed up over the situation that he couldn't even eat. Gesturing wildly as he talked to me, his tie fell into his cold soup.

Without revealing my own charismatic position, I explained to Bob that prayer meetings had been springing up all over the country. "At these meetings," I explained, "countless numbers have come to a wonderful experience of a saving relationship with Jesus Christ. It's a relationship that really makes life worth living. Instead of being dull, drab and monotonous, life becomes a joy because you start living for Christ, and not for yourself." I paused before asking, "Bob, have you ever wanted to live totally for Christ? Would you like to know the peace and the joy of this relationship with Jesus Christ?"

"I suppose I would," he replied, "but not now. I have enough to do just to square things away at home. This wife of mine needs medical attention and I want to see that she gets it. What advice would you give me about her?"

I told Bob that I would have to see Denise myself before making any judgment.

Rather hesitantly, Bob asked, "Are you sure that you want to get involved in this situation with my wife? Do you think that you can do anything?"

"*I* can't do very much," I answered, "but I know Someone who can." We then prayed together;

"Dear heavenly Father, we come to You in this special need. We ask You to give Your peace, Your love, Your joy, and Your wisdom to Bob that he might walk according to Your statutes. Draw him,

Lord, to the fountain of Living Water that he might know Jesus in a saving relationship. Give us light that we might know Your perfect will in this situation. We ask this in Jesus' name. Amen."

Bob was noticeably distressed that we had prayed aloud. Still, he was pleased that I was willing to help him in any way that I could. He gave me his phone number and address and invited me to drop by some evening within the next few days. He promised to tell Denise as little as possible about our secret meeting and our conversation.

Two days later, I went to Bob and Denise's home during the early evening. When I called in advance to tell them I was coming, Bob was the one who answered the phone. However, when I arrived, Denise answered the door bell. The door swung open and a beautiful lady with a splendid smile welcomed me into her house with the words, "Praise Jesus! I have prayed for such a long time that a real man of God who loves Jesus would come to my home. And now it's come true!"

This was Bob's fanatical wife, Denise, whose insanity he wished me to affirm, I laughed to myself?

Bob was standing in the arch between the hallway and living room. "See what I mean," he said nervously, referring to Denise's enthusiastic greeting. Discouraged, he walked into the back room to allow me some privacy with Denise so that I might make my evaluation of her condition.

As we began to share, Denise and I discovered that we were kindred spirits. We had a oneness and fellowship in Christ that was a special blessing to me. She impressed me as being a very solid and stable Christian. As she continued to share what the Lord had done for her, I discovered that she had been praying for months that Bob

16

would come to know Jesus as his Lord. Then, with a radiant smile, she shared her testimony of a transformed love for her unbelieving husband.

"I love this husband of mine," Denise began, "even though he has been unfaithful to me. It used to be the most severe defeat for me to know that he had a girlfriend. His obscenities, too, would make my whole being shudder. For months I had nothing to live for. Until I came to know Jesus as my Savior, I was a spiritual wreck. The house was a mess and I had no one to turn to. But now, with Jesus, I have victory. I know in my heart that Bob will know Jesus soon like I do!"

I listened eagerly as Denise continued to share what was on her heart. "I loved Bob when I first met him and took him as my husband; then he failed me through infidelity. After giving this failure to Jesus, I asked Him to place within me His perfect love for Bob that I might love my husband with a godly love since my own love was lacking. Praise Jesus, for He did just that. I love Bob more deeply now than I did when I first met him. I think it scares him because he knows I love him that much. With this godly love," she added, "I am ready to make any sacrifice for Bob that God wants of me, even if it means waiting years for his conversion."

I knew immediately that Denise was speaking of agape love—the love of God that takes over where our love fails.

Bob remained in the back room as Denise and I continued our sharing. She felt strongly that my coming to her home was a sign from the Lord that Bob would be converted to Jesus soon. We rejoiced in the wonderful assurance God had given to her, singing a verse of "Amazing Grace" together, with hands lifted to the Lord.

Hearing the singing, Bob emerged from the back room and sat down beside his wife. Denise started serving coffee and I knew that it was time for me to reveal my identity as a Spirit-filled Christian believer to Bob. I shared with him how I had discovered a personal relationship with Jesus through a dope addict who had given his life to God. I explained what this relationship meant to me and how it changed my life from one of pretense to one of dedication and victory in the ministry. Very carefully, I explained the difference between knowing *about* Christ from a textbook and actually *knowing* Him in an intimate way. I clarified for Bob that the wonderful experience of the baptism in the Holy Spirit was God's gift to His people in these latter days.

Eyeing me suspiciously, Bob asked, "Does all this mean that you become a fanatic?"

"No," I assured him, "you are never asked by God to do anything embarrassing to yourself or to others, for our God is a perfect gentleman."

Bob sighed with relief, although he appeared confused by it all. I knew by the concerned expression on his face that it was going to take more to convince him.

We never did get around to the task for which Bob had invited me to the house—confirming Denise's insanity. At that point, I'm not quite sure whether Bob thought my sanity was intact either!

I had certainly seen no evidence that there was anything wrong with Denise. What had became increasingly clear, however, was that Bob's heart was crying out for the same peace and love from Jesus that his devoted wife had received a year earlier. Before leaving their house, I prayed with them;

"Dear heavenly Father, we ask You to bless this house and we consecrate it to Your care. Please bless Bob and Denise in a special way. Bring them together in a bond of love and unite their hearts that

they may be one in mind, one in spirit, one in affection and one in Jesus. We ask this with confidence, in Jesus' name. Amen."

Before I left, Bob and Denise invited me back to their house to meet some of their friends on the following night. Earlier, Denise had told me that one of the couples coming was considering wife-swapping, better known as "swinging" in the suburbs. Denise had confided in me with the hope that I might witness to them about Jesus and His wonderful forgiveness. She already had the assurance that Bob would soon be saved, so her concern was for the salvation of the couples who were planning to visit her house for cocktails.

Four couples came for a party the following night, and I arrived at the same time they did. Denise greeted all of us at the door with a big smile. I was dressed casually like everyone else and was introduced simply as Joe. Conversation was informal as everyone socialized. Bob was laughing heartily at a dirty joke one of his friends had just told him.

Denise was so convinced that God was going to do something special that evening that she poured all the liquor down the drain and brought out glasses of coke for refreshment. Surprisingly, there was little reaction from the crowd or from Bob as Denise served the soft drinks. When she handed me my glass we both whispered enthusiastically, "Praise God!"

Yes, God did have something special prepared for us that night and it was as much of a surprise to me as it was to the others. Everyone was surprised—except for Denise—she was *expecting* a miracle! The cocktail party was miraculously transformed into a prayer meeting by the power of the Holy Spirit. Denise and I gave our testimonies of how Jesus became real in our lives. After prayer and singing, I extended the invitation to all to receive Jesus that very night. Several people responded, including the couple that previously wanted to become swingers.

To my surprise and joy, the last one to request prayer for salvation was Bob. I never saw such a strong-looking man cry so much while saying the sinner's prayer with me. He prayed with all his heart;

"Dear Lord Jesus, I come to You with the knowledge that I am a sinner. I realize now that You really died and rose again to rescue me from my sins. I ask for Your forgiveness. Come into my heart, Jesus, and fill me with Your peace and perfect love. In Your name. Amen."

As we all clasped hands to form a prayer ring around Bob, I noticed that every head was bowed except Denise's. Her smiling face was lifted upwards as she thanked God for keeping His promise of salvation for Bob.

And in that moment, the Lord clearly showed me that salvation came to a man that night, not because of a converted priest, nor because of a successful prayer meeting. No, salvation came to that man because of God's powerful, healing agape love pouring forth from the depths of his wife.

God's perfect love had healed a broken home!

AGAPE LOVE

GIVES COURAGE

Rhoda was in her mid-forties, the mother of seven children. She lived with her family in western Connecticut where her husband, Tom, was a truck driver. Together, they enjoyed a personal relationship with Jesus, and led a weekly Bible study for teenagers in their home.

I met Tom and Rhoda and their pastor at a businessmen's prayer breakfast a few years ago and was invited to their church to share my testimony. I found their church was charismatic, alive with the presence of the Holy Spirit.

After church, I was invited to Tom and Rhoda's home for fellowship. Then, they invited me to speak at their young people's Bible study the following week. Rhoda explained that the young adults represented many different churches as they gathered each Wednesday evening for prayer, sharing and song. Rhoda played the accordion, and I was invited to bring my banjo along to the next meeting.

Tom and Rhoda's Bible study on Wednesday evenings was the big event of the week. Rhoda would bake brownies and cakes and prepare sandwiches for the hungry teenagers who came. Her home was open to all and her heart was full of love. All the kids loved Rhoda,

too, and really appreciated her compassion and understanding.

Usually, Tom and Rhoda would lead the Bible study
themselves as well as the singing. Occasionally, they
would have a guest speaker bring the message of salvation
to the young people who had gathered for the meeting.

The house was packed with kids the night I arrived to
speak at the Bible study. I could barely get in the door as
Tom greeted me with, "Welcome to the Lighthouse, Joe."
I entered the front door amid the sounds of lively
conversation and loud laughter and shook hands with a
few of the young people who were aware that a stranger
had just walked in. Rhoda was in the kitchen with some of
the teenage girls preparing lemonade. "Make yourself
comfortable, Joe," she called. "We'll be starting very
shortly."

I tuned up my banjo as the young people gathered in
the living room. Some were sitting in chairs and others
were on the floor. Every available space was occupied as
more kids came than were expected. Tom introduced me
to the group and we began singing the Psalms. The house
was filled with heavenly music and the presence of the
Holy Spirit was manifest in a beautiful way in this home
consecrated for the Lord's work. During the course of the
meeting, several teenagers shared testimony of what Jesus
had done for them.

"I used to be a heavy pot smoker until I accepted Jesus
as Lord in my heart a few weeks ago," one young man
said. "Now, I know what it means to be high with Jesus."

"Praise God!" everyone shouted.

Another boy said, "It has been hard for me to be a
Christian, especially at school. I don't fit in with the old
crowd anymore. As long as I can come here to Rhoda's
house, I don't feel so bad. But, with all the booze and

drugs available in my school, I never thought I'd become a stranger to that environment."

A teenage girl added, "There is a small group of us at school who get together for prayer before classes start early in the morning. We pray daily that a spiritual revolution will happen to all the kids there, just like it's happening to us in this house."

Together, we prayed for one another as well as for all the schools represented. As we continued sharing before our Bible lesson, I observed that there were as many types of kids as there were voices. Some appeared straight-looking and others not. But, the important thing was that, other than a few newcomers, most of these young people were vibrant, new Christians who had surrendered their lives to Christ. It was heartwarming to see the joy that was expressed in their faces.

I began my talk that evening by throwing out a loaded question. "Would anyone like to tell us where he would be tonight if he weren't here and didn't have Jesus in his heart?" I was skeptical about their willingness to answer. Some began to laugh nervously, but, to my surprise, many volunteered answers that were candid and honest.

"If I weren't a Christian," one boy confessed, "I'd be getting drunk at my old buddy's house. That is all we did during the first two years of high school."

"I'd be getting high in my bedroom, listening to rock music and smokin' grass," another boy volunteered.

"Yah, me too," other voices agreed in unison.

"If I weren't a Christian, I'd be out parkin' with my boyfriend. Instead, we both have come here to praise God," one girl said softly as her hand clasped the hand of the boy next to her.

"Parents simply don't know all the things that their kids are doing these days," another girl spoke frankly. "It would really flip them out if they knew."

We continued with the Bible lesson after the sharing. The topic of our lesson was God's wonderful agape love. As we read from the last verses of the seventeenth chapter of John's gospel, we examined our responsibility to love others, even our enemies, as God first loved us. The young teenagers admitted to their failures in love, especially with their parents. One of the boys who spoke earlier said to the group, "I have a harder time loving my parents than I do those who persecute me at school for my belief in Christ." At my suggestion, we all bowed our heads after the Scripture lesson and took a moment to consider those whom we had a hard time loving.

Then we prayed;

"Heavenly Father, we thank You that You loved us even while we were sinners. Thank You for this new life in Christ. We ask You tonight to place in each of us Your agape love that we might love our enemies with Your love. We ask this in Jesus' name and we ask it with confidence. Amen."

Surrounded by a circle of joyous and loving teenagers, five newcomers made a commitment to Christ that night. They were united in God's love, and the Bible study in Rhoda's house was an opportunity to gather strength for the demands of the Christian walk.

These young people had really been blessed by hearing the teaching on agape love. One of the boys told me after the meeting, "I never heard that teaching before. Thank you very much for coming." I assured him that the entire teaching was scriptural. Then, I told him how I had also been blessed at the meeting and that I, too, had more to learn about putting agape love into practice in my *own* life.

While Rhoda and the girls were serving refreshments,

Tom pointed out a young man sitting on the floor who had many problems. "We can't seem to do anything for this boy," he told me. "His name is Jeff and he says he's an atheist 'though he comes faithfully every week to the meeting. However, he does not join in with the rest of the kids in singing and praying. We know he is still involved in drugs and has a police record for narcotic violations. He's very difficult to talk to."

I walked over to Jeff and asked him if he was a Christian. He answered that he wasn't. Then I asked him why he came to Tom and Rhoda's house. His answer convinced me that God's love was in full operation there.

"I come here because Rhoda is a beautiful person," he said. "She truly loves us kids and I like to be around people like that."

Although Jeff didn't want prayers said on his behalf, I knew that he wouldn't be without Christ for long in an atmosphere as Christian as Tom and Rhoda's home.

After everyone left that evening, Rhoda, Tom and I remained in the prayer room to pray for Jeff, anyway. We prayed that God's love would be made known to him through Tom and Rhoda in even fuller measure and that he might come to salvation. This young man had proven to be a little test for Rhoda in the past, standing out like a sore thumb at her prayer meetings.

I parted company with them after our prayer, promising to keep in touch. Rhoda thanked me for the teaching on agape love and invited me to return again soon. Little did she know that she would have her first big test of agape love the following week.

Rhoda was home alone one afternoon; her spirits were high as she sang while working. She was doing her spring cleaning when the sound of the vacuum cleaner was interrupted by the ringing of the telephone. The woman's voice on the other end was harsh and gruff.

"Are you the person who has the Bible study at your home on Wednesday nights?" she asked menacingly.

"Why, yes," Rhoda answered timidly.

The woman on the telephone growled, "I just found out that my daughter has been going to your house on Wednesday nights, and I'm furious."

"I'm awfully sorry that she didn't tell you," Rhoda replied.

The caller returned angrily, "You should be sorry, and you *will* be sorry when I'm through with you. My daughter isn't allowed to go to Protestant meetings. It's against our religion. I'm a Catholic and I just talked with a priest about it and he says it's not allowed. You have a lot of nerve, holding meetings for people who don't belong there."

Rhoda became tense. She'd never heard anyone so angry and so determined to speak her mind. "Our meetings are for everyone who wants to come," Rhoda explained. "We aren't trying to convert anyone to any religion. My husband and I are merely trying to bring the young people to Christ."

At this, the woman became angrier. "Who are you to set yourselves up as authorities about Christ?" she demanded. "Why don't you leave that to the pastor of your church, where it belongs?"

Trying to reason with her, Rhoda said, "Many of our young people don't go to church on Sunday. And besides, we can't expect the pastor to do all the work of bringing our kids to maturity in Christ, can we?"

"You mind your own business," the caller snapped back abruptly. Then, she threatened, "I'm coming down there to your house, and you better have a good explanation of what's going on when I get there, or else you're in serious trouble." The phone clicked and the angry woman was on her way to confront Rhoda face to face.

Rhoda was scared. She had never been the cause of such fierce anger before. For a moment, she panicked, and considered locking all the doors and calling the police. She was afraid that there might be a terrible scene. Rhoda's mouth became dry as she realized that her caller might harm her physically, so she went to the sink for a quick glass of water. Just above the sink was a scripture quotation that literally jumped out at her. It was from the book of Romans, "For I am not ashamed of the gospel of Christ, for it is the power of God unto salvation."

Rhoda went to the prayer room. From the window, she could see that the angry woman was on her way. She walked briskly like a Prussian general and her six-foot son followed behind her. Trembling, Rhoda fell to her knees in prayer. Remembering the Wednesday night lesson about how God's love takes over where ours leaves off, she prayed fervently.

"Dear Lord," she cried, *"I don't know this woman and I'm scared. Place in me Your agape love for her so that I may be Your instrument of love. Give me the right words to say. Take this nervousness and fear from me and give me peace in this impossible situation. I ask this in Jesus' wonderful name."*

Just then, the doorbell rang and Rhoda opened the door. The angry woman stood there with a scowl on her face and said, "Okay, now, you just tell me what's been going on at those Bible studies."

Summoning her courage, Rhoda said, "I am so happy

to meet you. It's a real pleasure for me to meet a woman who cares where her daughter is at night. Won't you come in for some tea?"

Surprised at the unexpected greeting, the woman stammered and finally said, "I won't have any tea, but I'll come in."

Her son waited awkwardly outside on the steps while his mother walked in and sat down in the parlor, still irritated.

"It was bad enough when my son married a Baptist girl," she complained. "It put the whole house into a tizzy."

Rhoda returned gently, "I knew just how you feel, because my daughter, a Baptist, married a Catholic boy."

With that as common ground, the two women began to talk, timidly at first and then with enthusiasm. Miraculously, God drew Rhoda and her caller into a wonderful unity and friendship that continues today. They were united through the blessed gift of agape love which was alive in Rhoda.

As a result of that love, this once distraught mother eventually came to the foot of the cross to give her life to Jesus. Today, her daughter continues to attend the Bible studies at Tom and Rhoda's house where God has seen fit to add strength and numbers to the meeting.

Another miracle of God's perfect love!

AGAPE LOVE

RESTORES MARRIAGES

While visiting in Minneapolis not long ago, I received a last-minute invitation to meet with a group of twenty married women who had gathered at the church hall for a Bible study. The group was a young mothers' social club that had decided to do something of a spiritual nature once a month. They had known each other for several years, and a mutual friend of ours had extended a somewhat belated invitation for me to come and speak to them. As a result, I didn't have much time to prepare my talk.

"Good evening, ladies," I began tentatively, in an attempt to get acquainted. "It's a pleasure to share with you this evening. I want to begin by commending you for making the supreme sacrifice of leaving your husbands and your children to come here tonight." By the sudden disapproving expressions on their faces, I could see that I had made a naïve assumption.

One of the women spoke up, "Are you kidding? That's why we left the house—to *get away* from our husbands!"

Again, I could see by their facial expressions that her words represented the feelings of the entire group. "My husband's a beast," another woman muttered in a low voice.

With that comment, all the women started laughing in

agreement. Not knowing whether to laugh or not, I ignored the comments and began to share my testimony of how Jesus became real to me as a person, after I had entered the ministry.

Happily, at the end of my sharing, we made a prayer circle and together prayed aloud as each woman made her own commitment to Jesus Christ as Lord. Then, the meeting continued with intercessory prayer as the women prayed for the needs of family and friends.

While listening to the prayer requests for their families, it became apparent to me that these women desperately needed to hear about agape love. Most of their conflicts were with their husbands and children. One woman prayed that her husband wouldn't be so hateful in the morning. Another one petitioned the Lord to straighten out her husband's drinking problem. Several others responded, "Mine, too."

I began to give the teaching on agape love, explaining very simply that God's agape love is power that helps us to love the unlovable and to forgive the unforgiveable. As I spoke, I began to sense a restlessness in my audience.

"No way," one of the women finally shouted. "You've got to be kidding about this love. I can't possibly love my husband after all he's put me through."

"That's just the point," I explained to her. "It is *in spite of* what your husband put you through that God's love makes it possible for you to love him anyway."

The women began to shrug their shoulders in disbelief. Here was a group of women who had been utterly frank about their problems with their husbands, and they were just as frank in expressing their disbelief about agape love. Finally, one woman said, "Okay, show us how it all works. Bring it down to the nitty-gritty. Do you mean to tell me that I'm supposed to stand there and take my husband's abusive speech?"

"Yes," I replied, "but not in your own strength."

"The secret to putting agape love to work," I continued, "is for all of us to become thermostats instead of thermometers. A thermostat remains steady while a thermometer moves up and down. The people who live with us are the very people whom God has placed there for us to love. But a thermostat is what we must become if we are to put agape love to work, especially in the home. We must stop reacting to the negative radar that comes at us. Quite literally, we must stop jumping up and down. We can let God control the situation in order for Jesus' wonderful love to come through."

The women became interested at that point, but most of them had quizzical expressions on their faces as their hands went up for questions. This was the first time that they had heard such a teaching on God's love.

One woman spoke up, "You'd have to be a kind of super person to live life without reacting."

"Boy, if I lived this thing that you're talking about," another said, "I'd be a saint and my family wouldn't recognize me anymore."

Still another woman responded, "My kids would think I was a weirdo if I changed the way I acted at home."

Finally, one woman admitted, "I have a hard enough time just *living* with my husband, let alone *loving* him."

It became clearer that evening, amidst the jumble of similar responses, that these women needed examples. I told them the story of Bob and Denise and how Denise was able to love Bob despite the jeering remarks and the callous treatment she received from him before his conversion. I explained that Denise was able to love Bob in spite of the fact that she knew that he was cheating on her.

One of the women remarked, "If I knew that my husband was cheating on me, I would divorce him."

"Exactly," I responded, "because you would be reacting just as the world reacts every time a crisis like that happens in a marriage. You would not be able to cope with infidelity precisely because you are loving your unfaithful spouse with your own diminished love." I continued to explain, "As we have seen from the story of Bob and Denise, God's love operating in Denise made it possible for her to cope with the problem. But, most importantly, it was God's love that cured Bob's problem of infidelity."

One woman interrupted bluntly, "Bob straightened up and converted to Christ because he knew he had a good thing in her."

"No," I answered firmly, "Bob straightened up because God's love in Denise was as overpowering as a huge machine that flattens cement. It was at the point where Denise's love failed and God's love took over that healing came for her husband."

I shared other stories of God's love with these women, especially of situations where agape love had healed a marriage. I explained again and again to them that the point of healing is the place where human love fails and where God's love begins. The women prayed in earnest that night in Minneapolis for agape love.

"Heavenly Father," we prayed, *"we thank You for bringing us together this night. We thank You for Your love and Your mercy. We come to You tonight with many problems in our homes. We are powerless to cope with the things that beset us there. We are asking You to give us Your agape love for*

this difficult, unruly, and unlovable member of the family. Let the power of Your love be made real in us that healing and blessing may come into our homes this night. We ask this in Jesus' name as we pray with confidence. Amen."

As we prayed, I noticed some of the women were crying and I rejoiced that God was touching and filling their hearts.

Four and a half months later, I received letters from several of them who reported that agape love was bringing the results for which they had prayed. One of them wrote:

"Dear Friend, I'm not one for letter writing, but I just had to tell you what happened to me.

"I was ready to throw away the whole idea you preached about God's love until something wonderful began happening in our home. When I returned from that glorious evening, I felt so free and loveable that I impulsively threw my arms around my husband—and accidentally stepped on his toes. He pushed me away and called me a clumsy fool. I told him I loved him and he answered, 'Why?'

"I began to cry that night because that ray of hope for a new marriage vanished. Maybe I was imagining things that weren't true. Maybe all this jazz about agape love is a lot of nonsense, I thought. But, as I began to pray, a great and wonderful peace came over me. My husband was asleep in the bed where I lay beside him. I knew that God was reassuring me in a new and marvelous way that I could love my husband better with *His* love. So, I prayed like I never did before. I talked to God in simple words, like a friend, and I asked for His agape love, in spite of the heartache that had already come my way.

"The next morning, I took special care preparing the

37

eggs and I made a batch of my husband's favorite muffins. I let him read the newspaper before I did, (usually I'd read the news section first and he'd read the sports). I prayed silently while he sat at the breakfast table. He looked at me strangely, sensing that I was not my usual self. He asked me if I was feeling okay and I reassured him that I was fine.

"After I saw him off to work and the children off to school, I sat on the sofa and did something I never do. I began to think back to our wedding day and how we had both consecrated our lives to one another. We had such hopes of living in harmony, but it wasn't long before disillusionment set in. He became cranky and I became domineering. It was the little things that destroyed our marriage, little arguments and petty disagreements. When I considered how blessed we were to have good health and a comfortable life, I wondered how we became so vicious toward one another.

"I realized that I began to make decisions for the house and the children and I know my husband resented not being included in on the activities at home. I could see him gradually withdrawing from the family and spending more time with his business interests. As I pondered our marriage over the years, I began to weep out loud in the living room, for God was showing me how I had failed at my end of the bargain, too. Somehow, I wanted that agape love more than ever. I knelt in our living room and I prayed with a new fervor and a new sense of purpose.

"Suddenly, the whole room filled with a glow and a beauty I had never felt before. God's wonderful hand was touching me in such a profound way. At that moment, I knew that life was going to be different for me and for my marriage. I started praying, 'Oh, God, please change me. Make me the bride worthy of Your love. Let this love

38

transform me and make me the wife and mother You want me to be. I know I have failed, but I want to do better.'

"My husband came home early that day because he had stomach cramps. I was delighted, although I wondered if the muffins had caused his problem. Anyway, I cancelled my appointment with the hairdresser and catered to my husband like never before. Later, lying on the bed with him I began to cry. He looked at me and asked why. I told him that I had been a rotten wife and that I was sorry for all the hurts I had caused him. I asked him to forgive me and he did. I told him that I forgave him for all the hurts he had caused me, too. We fell asleep crying in each others arms; his tears made me love him all the more.

"What a joyful moment it was when we lay there together as if cleansed from spots that had been ingrained for years. I prayed, 'Thank You, Lord, for this wonderful moment.'

"As the weeks and months have passed, my husband and I are more conscious of each other's feelings. Our marriage has been revitalized. We both feel it strongly. Whenever the children have a problem or need permission, I send them to their father. This is a whole new experience for them, but I can see that they have more respect for him. And, we do things as a family now.

"I'm a doubting Thomas by nature, so let me assure you that this agape love *does* work and *has* worked for me. I know we have a long way to go, but our daily prayers for courage and strength are answered. When I have difficult days, now, I have a wonderful resource in prayer.

"Please share this letter with anyone who needs it. Let other women know that God's love works miracles.

Thank you again for coming to us. Yours in Christ, Marcia."

From the same group, I received other letters attesting to the miracles which came about through the exercise of agape love. Another letter reads:

"Dear Servant of the Lord, Your coming to us was so surprisingly sudden and your message was so different that I was very skeptical throughout that whole evening. The story of your conversion to Christ sounded believable, but the teaching on God's love seemed strange. I always thought that love had to come from within you, that it was a question of whether you had it or didn't have it.

"Although I didn't *feel* love for many people, I offered my services at the hospital and nursing home whenever I could. I always was one who thought actions spoke louder than words. However, I never had any deep feelings for others. I just tend to be very unemotional by nature. But, you said that it was possible to have God's agape love by just asking for it. Never having known anything beyond the friendship one experiences through socials and card parties, I find that after asking for this agape love daily, I am feeling more love for others.

"While at the hospital visiting a friend of mine, who was experiencing much physical pain, I started to cry with a great compassion and love for her. It really comforted her that I seemed to care so much. Yet, I don't believe it was a question of my own compassion, for crying is not my nature. Rather, it was God's powerful force of love working in and through me that made me feel this compassion.

"My son-in-law notices a warmth in me that was not there previously. We have been drawn closer, too.

"May I close by saying that my life has been going

through such marvelous changes. I'm so happy and grateful to God that now I can not only bring *myself* to others and do little things for them, but I can bring Jesus *Himself* and His perfect love!

"May God protect and bless you. Our group prays for you daily. Sincerely in Christ, Marian."

AGAPE LOVE

SAVES

Several years ago, long before the other stories in this book occurred, I discovered the personal meaning of agape love in a dramatic way.

The mother of a heroin addict called me on the phone one Monday afternoon pleading with me to help her son. "I know my son too well," she cried in despair. "I know that he'll kill himself unless someone helps him. Peter has been on heroin for two years and I prayed that he would just come home. He's home now, but I don't know how long he can hold on before he'll run out and shoot up again."

I hung up the phone that day with a real feeling of helplessness, for even though I was already in the ministry, at that time I did not have a personal relationship with Jesus Christ. And, without fully understanding what Christ's act of agape love on the cross meant to me, personally, there was no way that I could give vital words of comfort and the encouragement of God's love to anyone else, no matter how desperately they needed it.

I remember the feelings of fear and helplessness I had that day very clearly. How was I going to help Peter, I questioned, when I wasn't really helping *anyone* who came to me for counseling. If I couldn't help people with much smaller problems than this, how could I possibly help free the chains that bound this young man in a pit of drugs and degradation?

For several months, I had gradually been losing interest in my vocation. In the counseling ministry, I was doing the work that I loved and for which I had been trained, and I should have been happy. But, I wasn't. Inside me there was an aching void, an unquenchable thirst. Something was definitely missing, though I didn't know what. I just wasn't getting the job done. I wasn't helping anybody. I discovered that the techniques in counseling I had learned did not work. Not for me, at least.

I was still feeling very low that afternoon when Peter came. He slouched in the doorway of the rectory, a long-haired, bearded young man, wearing jeans and a sport shirt. His eyes were red and tears were streaming down his cheeks. He looked every inch the picture of grief and despair as he reached out to me.

"Brother," he rasped, "I'm at the end of my rope and I'm pulling at straws. I need to know that there is something to live for. The only reason I'm here to see you today is because my old lady asked me to come. But, I have no hope. I don't trust anyone, and time is running out."

With those sobering words, Peter made his way from the entrance hall of the rectory to the parlor and slouched in a rather large armchair, moaning and crying while holding his sides in anguish. He looked like someone who was suffering from the intense pain of kidney stones. He cried for about a half an hour while I wondered how in the world I was going to tackle this problem.

What were the words that this broken human being needed to hear to be released from the bondage that gripped him? Did I have them? Did *anyone* have them? My mind raced as I stalled for time. One thing I knew for sure; if there was ever a time that I really had to help someone—this was it! Peter's desperate cries for help were pulling at something inside of me. It was as though I was the only person who could rescue him.

I vowed to myself right then that I would not try to fake my way through this. I was determined that even if I had nothing to do or say to help him, I would not wear my usual mask of security, hiding behind pious platitudes.

Yet, the prospect of having a suicide on my hands was one of the most frightening I had ever faced. I could not live with myself if I thought that I was somehow responsible for another human being's death. As best as I could, I assured Peter that I was genuinely interested in him and that I would be able to spend more time with him on the following day. He left after an hour, just barely comforted by the thought that I was interested in helping him.

That night, I phoned a friend who had a ministry to hardened addicts. He warned me that there was really nothing that I could do for Peter, and recommended that I get him to a hospital because he needed medication. Throughout the night I was unable to sleep, restlessly pondering what my friend had said and wondering how I should approach Peter's problem.

The next morning finally came, and it wasn't long before Peter appeared at the house as scheduled. He asked me if I would take him for a drive in my Mustang. When I asked why he wanted to go for a drive, he answered slowly; "The only time I can ever remember being close to God and at peace was when I was little and my folks would take me up to the lake, about an hour's drive north of here."

Without any further questioning, I reached for my keys. But, even then, I had no hope for a solution to Peter's drug problem and no idea what the outcome of this day would be. Little did I realize that I was about to see my first example of God's transforming agape love.

We got into the car and headed north toward Lake Crescent. On the way, Peter began to talk in a low voice, in a stream-of-consciousness fashion—a monologue that lasted the whole hour's drive to the lake. His words clearly revealed his feverish search for meaning and truth.

"All my life," he began slowly, "I've been searching for love and for peace. I grew up in the ghettos of San Francisco where I lived among the blacks. I learned to appreciate their struggle at an early age. I'm really into the blues music that they made famous. It's very sad music because they are very sad people. I learned how to play the harmonica from them. It always bugged me that the whites hate the blacks so and the blacks hate the whites.

"Our family moved to Seattle when I was still young. I served in church as an altar boy, but church never meant anything to me. I could never get over the prejudice of the Christians I met there; it seemed to be such a contradiction.

"I was a very restless kid, and that got me into trouble with my teachers. I would fool around in the library, throwing books and goofing off in the corridors. By the time I was a freshman in high school, I was drinking cough syrup to get high. Then, I began smoking pot on a regular basis. By the time I was a senior, I experimented with heroin.

"I went into the Marines to prove to the world that I was a man. In the service, I was hooked on heroin within nine months. I shot it into my body in ways that no one could see what I was doing. I put the needle between my

48

toes and under my tongue. When I got deathly sick, they gave me an honorable discharge and never even realized that my illness was caused by drugs.

"After my discharge from the Marines, I began to wander through most of the states on the west coast. By this time, I was a hardened addict with an enormous habit to support. I had to hustle in every way you could think of to get the next fix. Twice, I got hepatitis from dirty needles.

"None of my companions in the drug world stayed with me for very long. We usually wound up ripping each other off. Some of my friends died from overdoses and others were sent to prison for pushing cocaine. I escaped a prison sentence, although I deserved what my buddies got; I was responsible for bringing large supplies of drugs into Seattle in the late sixties.

"But, now, I have hit rock bottom. I doubt if I can ever come out of this pit I'm in. I feel like I'm in a cellar with a wall of cement over my head."

Peter's honesty was brutal and his story frightening. I had to remind myself that this was not make-believe. The long-haired companion in the front seat of my car was real and his story was a true flesh-and-blood chapter in his life. It seemed more like a tragic novel. More than ever, I was faced with the urgent need to give Peter words of encouragement and hope. Yet, I did not want to be phony, knowing he would see right through me. This young man had to have a reason to go on living, and it was up to me to help him find it.

There was just one problem—I had nothing to give him.

At the lake, we left the car, and I followed Peter down a trail that was familiar from his youth. As we came to the edge of the water on that beautiful fall day, Peter sat down on a tree stump with his head slumped over his arms. He began to cry, moaning deeply in despair and holding on to his sides as he did in the rectory. I sat helplessly a few yards away from him on a log. My mind was racing and I felt my pulse quicken. But, I had nothing to give to Peter, who sat comfortless in his agony. I had nothing to say to him. After a long and deadening silence, Peter looked up at me and asked very simply, "Brother, will you pray for me?"

Pray for him! Prayer was the furthest thing from my mind. At that time, I had never prayed out loud for anyone before. The only time I ever prayed in public was during the church services. The truth was that I had little faith in prayer. But, I prayed, anyway, not with the faith to believe a miracle was possible, but because Peter had asked me to. Yet, somehow, Peter had faith that day for he muttered a simple prayer that was to bring a miracle into his life. The prayer was said in all sincerity, and with more faith than even I, the priest, could muster.

"Lord," Peter cried out softly, *"if You really are real, if You really are what You say You are, show Yourself to me."*

We sat in silence for a moment. Then, I watched in amazement as a smile slowly crossed Peter's face, transforming the lines of anguish into channels of joy. His shoulders relaxed and his hands dropped away from where they had been clutching his sides. With tears in his eyes, Peter stood to his feet.

"I feel a strange sense of peace," he said quietly. "I feel as though God has just given me what I've been looking for. Somehow, I know that there really is hope for me, in spite of what I've done. I *know* that God is with me."

Something had really happened to Peter! Not understanding, I actually thought that he was hallucinat-

50

ing. But, Peter assured me that what he was feeling had nothing to do with drugs. "I've never felt like this before," he sighed. "I feel so light inside—so free."

Then, he knelt down and confessed his sins before His Maker, pouring out his heart and weeping more tears of joy.

The atmosphere had changed in an instant. The mood was light, almost jovial, on the trip home. Peter sang and played his harmonica for me. There was an overwhelming sense of hope on the horizon for my young companion. But, when I left Peter off at home and drove on to the rectory, I began to doubt the validity of all that had happened, wondering how long what I believed was only Peter's "feeling of elation" would last.

Early the next morning, the phone rang. It was Peter's mother on the other end of the line, talking so excitedly through her tears that I could hardly understand her.

"Ohhh...th-thank you, Reverend Manning," she cried. "My husband and I can't thank you enough for what you have done for our Peter. Something is different with him—I can tell. And, he has never been able to go two days without drugs like this before! Thank you!"

I hung up the phone with those feelings of inadequacy and guilt rising again. I knew that *I* didn't deserve any thanks for what had happened. I didn't even *understand* what took place at the lake—and I was in no way responsible for the sudden change in Peter's life.

For many days after, Peter was locked in his room suffering because of withdrawal from the heroin. Each day, I called him on the phone to find out how he was doing and he would answer, "Brother, Jesus is real. He is helping me. I know that His strength through prayer is the very thing that has lifted the cloud of heroin from my head. I can think clearly, now, and my hands are steady.

I've been reading the Bible, too. It's real heavy stuff."

It was apparent to me that Peter had a very real encounter with Jesus Christ. Yet, I was actually too embarrassed to say the name of Jesus to him as he would so often to me. Sometimes, during our telephone conversations, Peter would lead the most simple and spontaneous prayer. It was somewhat awkward to be on the receiving end. Still, I could not deny the fact that Peter had been genuinely touched by a higher power, the Source of which I had not yet tapped in my own life.

Finally, after several weeks, Peter showed up at the rectory again, completely recovered from drugs. His face glowed and his eyes were clear and bright for the first time since I had met him.

"Brother," he said joyfully, "I have given my whole life to Jesus and He has changed me. He has given me this tremendous desire to tell others about the peace He can give. Thanks for helping me, and for being there when I needed someone."

With that last remark, the feeling of helplessness I felt the first time I met Peter welled up again. Something was missing from my life—what was it?

Meanwhile, with a new frame of mind and a vibrant faith, Peter set out to "conquer the world." He walked the streets of Seattle and witnessed to his friends about the new peace that was his through Christ. He did not have to talk much to convince his onlookers, for Peter radiated peace and love. Where formerly he was restless and paranoid, not trusting a soul, suddenly Peter was reaching out to his old friends and to strangers with a love that God had placed in him through the Holy Spirit.

He began visiting the rectory with a long line of young people who had recently been drawn to Christ through him. He would bring his new disciples to me that I might approve of their spiritual progress. However, I felt like a child at a circus, very much apart from the activity in the ring. I could only give half-hearted approval to the success Peter was enjoying in the street ministry. I still could not really say "Jesus" as he could, even though I was the one with the degree in theology, and I couldn't join in his exclamation of "Praise the Lord" with equal enthusiasm. The truth was that I was a pretender. My heart was seeking the very fulfillment that Peter had found. I merely had head knowledge about Jesus Christ and this was not solving my own problems, nor was it solving the problems of those who came to the rectory for my help.

Not long afterwards, Peter was invited to give an assembly at a local church high school, to relate his experiences with drugs and how dangerous they are. He invited me to come to this assembly to give him moral support, and I agreed. Hundreds of students were gathered in hushed silence as they listened attentively to the testimony of this reformed drug addict. Peter boldly told them how the Lord had delivered him from drug addiction and given him a freedom he had never known before.

He spoke in simple words to the students about the peace that the Lord gives when you make a total commitment of your life to Christ, allowing Him to change your heart. With glowing enthusiasm, Peter invited the students to make a commitment to Christ that very afternoon in the assembly hall of the high school. I watched from the rear as a couple hundred students went forward to make their peace with God by receiving Jesus as Lord of their lives.

I left the school in a hurry that day, filled with the remorse of a Judas who had become a servant of God under false pretenses. I returned to the rectory and went straight to my room, hurting for the very life that I was lacking, in desperate search for the peace that only Christ can give. There was an aching void inside me that I just couldn't understand.

And then, one Sunday morning as I lay awake at five o'clock, it was as if a curtain opened wide, revealing my own spiritual condition. Outwardly, I was a devout minister of God, but inwardly I saw that I was a phony, arrogant, and a selfish sinner. I had come to the end of myself at last. I knew what I needed to do and I did it eagerly, praying like I had never prayed before.

"Dear Lord, I want to be Your servant and Your priest. I want to stop being a phony, pretending to know You. I ask You to come into my heart this day and to take over my life. I confess my sins and shortcomings to You, asking for Your forgiveness. Please give me Your peace and Your wonderful love. I want Jesus to be my Lord and Savior and I will walk with Him, no matter what happens, as long as I live."

Life has not been the same since that day. When I invited Jesus into my heart, I became a new creature, just as the Bible promises. And now, I don't just talk about the power-supply, I'm tuned into the *Source*, Jesus! No longer do I *counsel* people with problems, I merely introduce them to Jesus who can heal their hearts and *solve* their problems!

A lady in Oregon, after hearing the story of my rebirth in Christ through the experiences of a drug addict, said to me, "Pastor Joe, do you realize the infinite, perfect love of God in your life that He would allow Peter to go through the worst kind of misery and despair in order to bring both of you to the fountain of Living Water?"

That was my first revelation of the beauty and power of God's agape love, and though it was several years ago, when I think of it, even to this day, I could shout it from the rooftops!

AGAPE LOVE

OVERCOMES RESENTMENT

Tony and Carla were an Italian couple who lived just outside New York City in a fashionable residential area. In their thirties, they were the parents of two children. I met this couple recently at a prayer meeting. Their story, however, begins long before that.

Tony and Carla were very materialistic. During the first ten years of their marriage, Tony had worked at eight different jobs, always striving for a salary that would exceed the previous, already substantial one.

Their home was a decorator's dream and the source of much pride and delight to its owners. Expensive and lavishly carpeted throughout, it was regally furnished in Italian Provincial and looked like a showroom model. Carla had a talent for arranging colors and patterns, and Tony's salary afforded many luxuries for them as well as for their children.

Carla enjoyed the frequent shopping trips she could make, adding a new blouse or dress to her already extravagant wardrobe. She also took the children out to lunch frequently. Tony patronized the most expensive stores and would think nothing of buying several two-hundred-dollar suits to hang in his already crowded closet. Their children, too, were well-groomed and well-dressed. In no way did the family suffer from lack of any material thing.

Tony and Carla were not churchgoers and neither of them had a personal relationship with Jesus Christ. The mere mention of religion was a sore point with them that always provoked arguments, especially when they were visiting relatives who did attend church. A distant cousin tried to coax Tony into attending a prayer meeting, but with no success, for Tony was as stubborn as a mule about religious matters.

One day, while at a family barbecue, Tony was cooking hamburgers when his brother-in-law, John, surprised him by asking if he would like to become partners in a new trucking freight business. Tony really liked John, who was married to his sister, Anna. And, Tony and Anna had had a very close relationship from childhood, growing up right next to each other in age in the midst of a large family. These factors made the business proposition very inviting for Tony from the start.

After a long discussion that assured him of a better salary than he already had, Tony heartily agreed to his brother-in-law's proposal. Cheerily voicing their approval, all the relatives joined in the celebration of the new partnership. Tony had made the decision to leave his ninth job in ten years for greener pastures.

Tony's flexibility and determination enabled him to adjust to the new business quickly, and he boasted that his salary was better than ever. Weeks rolled into months, and the business was really getting off the ground. Tony and John were immensely pleased with the progress and profits, and so were their wives. The two couples met together frequently to celebrate the growth of their successful partnership. At these gatherings, Anna admitted that she was just as proud of her younger brother, Tony, as her own husband. Anna's love for Tony was special and she was sure that nothing could ever change it.

Then, one rainy day, John and Tony were delivering large boxes to the shipping section of a factory when Tony accidently lost his footing at the end of the truck and fell backwards onto the wet pavement. He was rushed by ambulance to the nearest hospital where they discovered that he needed immediate surgery. His spine was broken and he had almost severed his spinal cord.

Requiring nine months of medical care, Tony was no longer able to work in the trucking business. His condition improved over that period of time, but the medical expenses still unpaid were overwhelming. Tony felt very strongly that the freight business should compensate for the lost time as well as pay the medical bills that required immediate attention. But, John and Anna disagreed, claiming that it would put too large of a dent in the budget. Hurt and angry, Tony and Carla broke off all business and personal relationships with them. Tony absolutely refused to have anything more to do with his sister who had hurt him so deeply. Disconsolate, Carla could not understand how Anna could be so cruel, refusing to help her own brother.

Tony and Carla really struggled to pay the bills that were facing them. He found a new job some distance from home and she got a job on the side to help out. Slowly, the tension grew in their home. After having the comforts and luxuries of suburban living for so long, they were now struggling for the very necessities of life. More and more often, Tony and Carla would argue because they were angry or overtired. Their children were no longer given the attention they were used to, and the house suffered from neglect because of commitments away from home.

Tension mounted to such a peak that Carla began to suffer increasingly from migraine headaches.

Though the bills were gradually brought under control at the cost of extreme personal sacrifices by both Tony and Carla, the silent wall of bitterness between the two families became so strong that it seemed nothing imaginable could tear it down. They never mentioned Anna's name in their house at all. Tony felt that he was the helpless victim, betrayed by his own flesh and blood. Not wanting to take sides, his parents withheld their opinions, which didn't help Tony's feelings of resentment at all. Tony and Carla's home became a morgue without the usual family get-togethers.

Then, one day, they were visited by Tony's Christian cousin, Michael, who had wanted them to attend prayer meetings in the past. The young man's joy and enthusiasm were a noticeable contrast to the gloom of their household. Regardless of Tony's religious feelings, Michael was welcomed as he spoke of the wonderful miracles and blessings at the prayer services in his church. Although Tony and Carla had no immediate favorable response to the idea of a prayer meeting, they did want to know how their cousin became so happy and optimistic.

With a little coaxing from Michael, and a lot of prayer as well, Tony and Carla were finally persuaded to attend a prayer meeting. In the midst of their misfortune and sadness, they invited Jesus Christ to come into their hearts and to take over their lives, realizing that He could change the gloom to gladness. That night, they received Jesus Christ as Lord and Savior.

Sometime later, I was invited to speak at the weekly prayer meeting that Tony and Carla now attended regularly. We became friends and I was invited to their home. As we began to share our personal experiences with each other, they told me of the accident and all the problems that had resulted. Then, they revealed the enormous wall of resentment that they had towards John and Anna. It was a perfect opportunity for me to share the power of agape love to heal and restore broken relationships and to mend broken hearts.

On his knees before God, Tony asked for and received forgiveness for his resentment of his sister and brother-in-law. Then, he asked God to fill him with *His* agape love for Anna whom he hadn't seen in two years.

A short time later, Anna's daughter became ill and was rushed to the hospital with a bleeding ulcer. Tony went with love in his heart to be reunited with his sister. As he entered the hospital room, Anna looked up at him and asked, "Why have you come? Is it because of my daughter?"

"Because of Jesus," Tony answered with a smile and an embrace, "and because, Anna—I love you."

Through the miracle of God's agape love, a brother and sister were gloriously united after two years' separation, and an entire family was restored! Today, Tony and Carla are filled with the love of Jesus. Their home is radiant with the fullness of the Holy Spirit and has been consecrated to the Lord's work.

No matter how deep the chasm of separation, or how high the wall of resentment, God's perfect love never fails!

AGAPE LOVE

CONQUERS DEPRESSION

Maria was an effervescent Christian woman in her late thirties, the mother of two teenage boys and the wife of a distinguished executive. They lived in a suburban section of eastern Long Island, in rather comfortable surroundings. Before I came to know this family personally, I knew Maria only as the woman at the prayer meeting with the big beautiful smile. She just glowed with the presence of the Holy Spirit even though she hadn't known Jesus as her Lord for a very long time. Those who knew her, spoke of her charm and warmth.

I was introduced to Maria a few months later, after one of the prayer meetings at which I was ministering. I discovered the same qualities in her that I had previously heard about. She appeared to be as beautiful on the inside as she was on the outside. After seeing Maria at the charismatic meetings each time I came to New York, I was invited to spend some time at her home. My relationship with Maria and her husband, David, became a close one. Whenever we came together for fellowship, we would always begin and end our times with prayer. Never did I leave their company without seeing the Lord's blessings. Most often, I was on the receiving end. Yet, the greatest blessing for me was the ever constant joy that radiated from Maria's face.

Maria's joy was infectious; her love for others really showed. Never did an opportunity pass when she wasn't telling someone about the wonderful love that Jesus had for them. "I'm just ready to explode with the love of Jesus," she said to me once. "Since I accepted Jesus into my heart I've had such an overpowering love for everyone. I feel so free and so alive. I've never known this freedom to love before now."

Whenever Maria traveled to the market or the shopping center, she would offer rides to long-haired hitchhikers along the way. She witnessed freely to her passengers about Christ's love and the joy of salvation. Even if some of those hitchhikers looked indisposed from drugs or alcohol, Maria continued the practice of her little shuttle service for the praise and the glory of God. She was clearly a woman on fire with the love of the Lord.

Then, tragedy struck. One day, not long after one of my visits, David, Jr., Maria's oldest son, was riding his bicycle along a country road. Within minutes after leaving his house, he became the victim of a hit-and-run accident. He was thrown thirty feet into the bushes, his body broken in almost every conceivable place. David, Jr. lay unconscious, his bicycle twisted beyond recognition. A passing motorist stopped and called an ambulance. It sped quickly to the grisly scene, rushing David, Jr. to the county hospital, where his life was hanging in the balance in the intensive care unit.

The horrible news of the accident reached David and Maria. They rushed to the hospital, where they were told by the doctor that there was a strong chance that their son would not survive.

Maria felt her life had caved in. As the distressed mother of a boy dying from a senseless accident, she was on the verge of a total collapse. In the meantime, the news of David, Jr.'s accident traveled throughout the area. Various prayer groups and churches began to pray unceasingly for his recovery. The Christians with whom Maria and David, Sr. shared fellowship were only too willing to help in any way they could. One of them called me long distance and told me the shocking news. I promised to drive down to be with the family as soon as possible.

That night, there was a team of nurses beside young David's bedside around the clock. His parents paced the corridor of the intensive care unit for hours. Though Maria knew others were praying, it was hard for her to pray, now. She had been taught in Bible study how important it is to pray and praise God in good times and in bad, but she never realized that things could ever get this bad. She was emotionally crushed as she turned to her husband in despair. Tearfully, Maria told him that if David, Jr. didn't pull through, she did not want to live, either. David, Sr. tried to comfort her, holding her in his arms as their son lay in the next room. They continued their tense vigil throughout the night.

At five A.M., David, Jr. miraculously regained consciousness. His parents were overjoyed. Yet, in spite of this happy turn, the attending doctor told them that their son would definitely require a long recuperation. He would not be able to move his muscles again without months of physical therapy.

The news was an added blow for Maria. She became increasingly angry at the hit-and-run driver as she considered the extent of David's injuries. Whoever the hit-and-run driver was, Maria felt that he had to be the cruelest person in the world to leave her son lying in such a broken condition, possibly to die! Her bitterness began to grow.

By the time I drove to New York to be with the family, David, Jr. had already been removed from the intensive care unit. His x-rays were completed and the grueling treatments begun. The doctor kept him under heavy sedation for the pain and placed him in an open ward of the hospital. I can clearly recall the grim picture of David, Jr. lying in his bed. He was in traction with plaster casts covering practically every limb of his body. His arms and legs were suspended in the air like a puppet with strings.

David and Maria greeted me by their son's bedside. David, Sr. was noticeably pleased that I had come, but I will never forget the defeated look on Maria's face. Formerly, she was the woman with the radiant smile and the joyous spirit. Now, she looked like a completely different person, a captive in a concentration camp! All her joy was gone. She was embittered by what had happened to her precious son. A hospital visit from a friend could do little to lift the spirits of this woman touched by a tragedy she had never known before. After a short visit, I returned home.

Maria's defeat and anger only deepened. She was furious with the doctors at the county hospital, convinced that they were not giving her son the attention he needed. The specialists at the hospital were in great demand, and they had only a minimum of time to be at David's disposal. Some days would pass when they would not see him at all.

Maria's bitterness spread like a cancer as the days melted into months. She was angry at God and at the people who encouraged her to pray. She was angry at the doctors who had no time for David and most of all, at the callous hit-and-run driver who had hurt her son so terribly.

Closing herself off completely from her Christian companions, Maria drew her blinds and removed the phone from the hook. She didn't wish to be bothered with anyone except her immediate family. Finally, young David was allowed to return home, provided a hospital bed was placed in his room. He continued with the long and tedious therapy treatments there. The months continued to pass and since David, Jr. required constant care, he occupied most of his mother's time. Now, she definitely believed she had a good excuse for neglecting letters and prayer meetings.

Actually, when Maria wasn't busy nursing her son back to health, she was feeding feelings of hate and resentment toward the hit-and-run driver. These feelings were strongest during many sleepless nights as she contemplated who the driver might be. She imagined that he was either an alcoholic or one of those long-haired drug users she used to drive to the store. If there was ever love for long-haired people in Maria's heart, she was sure that it was gone forever.

Finally, after months of recuperation, David, Jr. was back on his feet and soon returned to school. Slowly, Maria began to realize how much time she had lost. Like a flower that had to learn how to bloom all over again, she began to painstakingly search for a way back to her old self.

At this time, I was invited to share my personal experiences with a charismatic group near Maria's home. During the evening, one of the women said to me, "Gee, I'm really worried about Maria. We haven't seen her for many months. She doesn't come to the prayer meetings anymore. She doesn't even answer the telephone when we call." Another concerned friend added, "Is there some way that you could visit her and find out how things are going? We sure would like her to know how much we love her and have been praying for her family."

After the meeting, I dropped by David and Maria's house. We greeted each other with a hug and they quickly told me the news that young David, Jr. was almost back to normal. (He was in the den looking at his rock collection.) We agreed that his recovery was truly a miracle and together we prayed;

"Thank You, Father, for this miracle of healing! You alone are the Author of life. We thank You that You gave David back the full use of his limbs. We praise You and thank You for all Your blessings, in Jesus' name. Amen."

After a warm cup of tea and a brief sharing of how they had suffered in the midst of the crisis, David and Maria invited me to stay the night. On the following morning, the sun was beaming through the windows. It was the beginning of a beautiful day. David, Sr. had to leave for work, so I arose just in time to say goodbye to him before he left the house. Meanwhile, downstairs in the kitchen, Maria was fixing some eggs. "Why don't we have breakfast on the picnic table outside," she called to me.

The birds were chirping as Maria poured hot coffee in my mug. Then, before even touching her food, she began to pour her heart out. Maria told me step-by-step the entire story of her personal nightmare and what God was saying to her through it all. She could hardly wait to tell me the important lesson that God was trying to teach her about His love.

"You'll never know the struggle I've had during these months of young David's recuperation," she said. "There were times I wished that the hit-and-run driver who hurt my David would be convicted and sent to jail. I actually wished him harm! There were many sleepless nights when the image of a long-haired hippie would haunt me. I never wanted to see another long-haired person again."

"What happened to the love that you used to have for those kids, and for people in general?" I asked her.

She responded sincerely, "I've asked God to forgive me and to restore me back to normal. The Lord has shown me what little love I really have on my own. It's humiliating for me to admit that I sometimes hoped that the hit-and-run driver were dead."

"What is your feeling now toward the driver?"

"I don't hate him like I used to," she answered, "but I know that the only way I can love him is with God's love. I cannot possibly love him in my own strength." Softly, Maria began to cry, "I've failed a big lesson and I want so much to be back in God's favor. I really want to love people with His love instead of my own."

After she wiped her tears with the table napkin, we joined hands together and prayed that God's love would be made real to her.

"Dear heavenly Father, we thank You for Your love and mercy. We thank You for forgiving our sins. We ask You to place in Maria Your love for this hit-and-run driver. May Your agape love become real to Maria in this situation, that she might love him with Your perfect love. Her heart is open to receive. We ask this together in Jesus' name. Amen."

Agape love was made real to Maria that day. Now, her life is a stronger testimony than before the accident of God's love in action. Together, she and her husband are planning a youth Bible study in their home to which long-haired drug addicts who seek Jesus are invited. Triumphantly, Maria has discovered that only in God's agape love is it possible to conquer depression and to truly love and forgive!

AGAPE LOVE

UNITES FAMILIES

I was working in a poverty program in New England the summer that I met Larry and Paula. Exhausted from the hectic pace of working with underprivileged children, I was glad the summer was finally ending. With time to rest shortly after the program ended, I was visited at my headquarters by a Christian couple from Maine whom I'd met earlier at a prayer meeting in New Hampshire. We had a happy reunion and they mentioned Larry and Paula whom they had known as neighbors in Florida and who now lived in Massachusetts.

These friends from Maine felt that I needed a change from the noise of the city. Since I had a week to spare, they called Larry and Paula and made arrangements for me to spend the time at a little cottage that still other Christian friends owned, on a lake not far from Larry's house. Together, we drove at night toward Massachusetts, arriving after midnight at Larry and Paula's. They'd been expecting us, and we sat up for hours sharing the things of the Lord.

Larry and Paula were people of average means. Larry was a shoe salesman and Paula was a wife and mother. They had two children, Bill and Sandra. Bill, the oldest, was a lively teenager, a high school dropout.

It was a real pleasure to meet these new Christians and

to be welcomed as a cherished brother on our first meeting. Two hours passed quickly, and at last someone suggested that we retire for the night. There was a spare bedroom for the other couple, but Paula informed me apologetically in her soft, southern accent that I would have to sleep in the same room with her son, Bill. I told her I didn't mind at all, and we all trudged wearily to our sleeping places. I didn't turn on the light in the room for fear that I would awaken eighteen-year-old Bill; rather, I just crawled into the other bed and went to sleep.

The sound of voices from the kitchen brought me out of my sleep the next morning. As I opened my eyes, I saw a long-haired boy in the other bed across the room from me. He was still asleep. For a few minutes I studied him as he slept, listening to the heavy sound of his breathing. Then, thinking I was doing him a favor, I woke him up.

"You've got nerve, sleeping this late," I commented jokingly as his eyes opened. "I work harder than you do, and I get up earlier, too."

Bill laughed. With that as an introduction, he began talking to me as he would talk to a special confidante. He explained that hassles with his parents had forced him to leave home about nine months before.

"My folks are really surprised to find me back home," he told me. "Actually, I came home because I was scared. I was climbing in the White Mountains of New Hampshire with my best friend, Gus. Boy," Bill sighed, "can he play a mean guitar. Well, anyway, we did some dangerous climbing. Gus is a real daredevil. We've done a lot of crazy things together."

"Did you have a close call?" I asked him.

"You'd better believe it!" he replied. "We climbed the slopes without proper gear. Gus led the narrow way and I followed. I almost fell twice and so did Gus."

As Bill lay in bed propped up on his elbows, he

continued with his story. I listened intently. "That's why I came home yesterday," he went on. "I thought my folks might be worrying about me."

As we began to talk about lighter things such as music and hitchhiking, I was aware that here was a boy who was lively as well as adventurous. I noted, too, how well we hit it off. There was a knock on the bedroom door that interrupted my thoughts. Bill's mom called out, "Are you up and at 'em?" "Yes, indeed," I answered for both of us.

I went to clean up and then head for breakfast while Bill got dressed in the bedroom. Morning laughter greeted me from the kitchen. The two couples were reminiscing about their days in the South as Paula prepared eggs, grits and bacon. "Praise the Lord," shouted Paula and the rest who had been waiting for us "slowpokes" to join them for breakfast. I met Bill's sister, Sandra, a pretty young blonde who appeared to be shy.

"Have you ever had grits before, Joe?" Paula enquired above the noisy chatter. I told her that I hadn't. "Then we're going to give you a little taste of southern hospitality," Larry chimed in, grinning broadly.

Finally, Bill came to the breakfast table and we all sat down to eat. Larry led with the prayer, "Dear Lord, we thank You for bringing us all together. And we thank You for this food. Bless it to our bodies' use and us to Your service. We ask this in Jesus' name. Amen."

We were famished, so we ate a hearty breakfast. The conversation was lively, like a gathering of old friends. I noticed, however, that Bill was a different person at the breakfast table than in the bedroom. Except for teasing his sister, Sandra, he remained tight-lipped throughout the meal. I sensed a tension between him and his parents. Each time one of them would speak, Bill would betray his irritation.

Having finished eating, I excused myself from the

kitchen and went into the parlor. Bill immediately followed. When he saw my banjo, he brightened. "Wow, is that yours?" Bill asked. He was delighted to know that I could play the instrument. "Play something," he added. While the folks were busy talking in the kitchen, I played two folk songs for Bill and he seemed really pleased. I explained that I brought the banjo along for the week because I needed to learn some new chords.

"My friend, Gus, plays the guitar like a rock star," Bill commented proudly. "We're gonna make a recording soon. I don't play, but I help Gus with the band."

When we reached a lull in our conversation, I rose from my chair. "I need to pick up some new banjo strings and take some clothes to the laundry before heading out to the cottage," I said to Bill. He wanted to come with me so I told Larry and Paula where we were going.

While he was driving my car through the heart of the city, Bill seemed to relax from the tension he felt at the house. He told me how he had wrecked his own car not too long before. It certainly sounded like my young friend had a lot going against him.

When we arrived at the shopping center, Bill pointed out all his old hangouts, including the pizza parlor where one of his paintings hung on the wall. He told me how much he liked to paint in his free time. We walked to the music store and then to the laundry, laughing and telling each other jokes as we waited for some time for the clothes to dry. Afterwards, at Bill's suggestion, we went to a large restaurant at the Mall to have a hamburger. We laughed at each other's amusing experiences and favorite stories.

Our laughter subsided as we headed back to the house. Breaking the silence, I asked Bill what he thought of Jesus Christ.

"Religion is a drag to me," he countered. "I've met

more hypocrites than you can imagine. Some churches won't let me and my buddies in because of our long hair. Do you think that's very Christian?"

I felt the need to tread lightly on the subject, so I didn't answer him.

"Right now," Bill continued, not noticing my silence, "life is a real bummer for me because I don't have a car or a job. My parents are always bugging me about my appearance. They think I look like a bum, but I wish they'd get off my back."

As we approached the driveway of the house, I asked, "Bill, what are your plans? Are you looking for a job?"

"Not just now," he answered. "Tomorrow, Gus and I plan to hitchhike out to California. I'll be gone for a couple of months." Before we joined the rest of the family, Bill turned to me and said, "Boy, I sure wish you could meet Gus. You sure would dig him."

While our visit ended rather abruptly, we had had a good time together. Bill really seemed to appreciate the fact that I was listening to him and enjoying him for who he was.

That afternoon I packed all my luggage back in the car again. It was time to go to the cottage on the lake for my rest. I said goodbye to Paula, Sandra and the couple from Maine, thanking them for everything. I said goodbye to Bill, wishing him a happy trip with Gus out to the west coast. Then, Larry led the way to the cottage. After making sure I was settled, he returned to his family in the city. With two and a half months of constant activity behind me, and only five hours sleep the night before, I slept like a log that first night.

The following day was restful. As silence encompassed the scenic atmosphere of water and trees, I began to unwind. I was alone in the cottage that provided the quiet

I cherished. I felt I needed this retreat from the problems of other people. Selfishly, I thought that I deserved the long-awaited rest. But, that very night, the phone rang. It was Larry.

"Joe," he began, "ever since you left Bill doesn't know what to do with himself."

"I don't know what you mean," I replied, perplexed.

"Bill cut the grass after you left," Larry continued, "but all day today he has been moping around the house. He seems lost."

Surprised, I said, "I thought that Bill was leaving for the west coast with his friend, Gus."

"Wait," came the answer, "I think he wants to talk to you himself."

Bill took the phone from his dad and said hello. He didn't have anything in particular to say. I asked him if his plans were called off for the trip to California and he answered that they had been. There was a short pause. In that silence, the Lord was telling me to invite Bill to the cottage.

"Would you like to come up to the cottage?" I asked him. He answered enthusiastically, saying that he'd be right up.

While awaiting Bill's arrival, I began praying to the Lord;

"Dear heavenly Father, I don't know what Your plan is for young Bill. You certainly are full of surprises. Give me Your wisdom in this situation. But, most especially, Lord, give me Your wonderful agape love that I might manifest Your love to this lost boy. I ask that Bill might come to know You. Help me, too, Lord, not to come on too strong with Your message. I ask this with confidence in the name of Jesus. Amen."

Bill smiled as I greeted him at the door. He was happy to be with me because he knew that I really cared about him.

We had a wonderful time together on the lake that week. Our recreation included boating, tennis, music, cookouts, and watching television. Although it was not the rest that I had anticipated, it was a precious time of fellowship and sharing. In more serious moments, Bill told me that one of the most crushing blows in his life came when his long-standing girlfriend broke off with him because her parents didn't like him.

In conversation one night at the cottage, Bill confided in me, "That was the hardest thing I've ever faced. When I lost my girl's love, my whole world caved in. I dropped out of school because I just couldn't face her in the corridors. Then, I left home because of the pressure from my parents to return to school. I lived in my buddies' cars during some of those cold nights. Finally, I got a part-time job, and then a cheap apartment. I was so lonely that I began to drink heavily and I really let myself go."

I told Bill that I understood the situation. Then, I assured him that if he would give everything to God, things would change. He didn't answer. "Bill," I went on, "a girl's love might change, but God's love is permanent. It never changes. God loves you more than you'll ever know."

He listened, but he was more intent on sharing his hurts just then. Bill just needed more time to think.

All too soon, our time together at the cottage on the lake ended. I said another goodbye to Bill and his family and thanked them again for their kindness toward me. It was a vacation that I would never forget.

Two weeks after I returned to my home, I received an invitation to speak at a prayer meeting that Larry and

Paula attended regularly in their area. To their great surprise and joy, as well as mine, their prodigal son, Bill, came to the prayer service with them. Formerly, he'd have nothing to do with "religion."

I didn't even recognize Bill at first because he had dressed up for the occasion. He told me that he came because of our friendship and because I was going to share testimony and song.

There was much joy, love and laughter at the meeting that night and I noticed that Bill, although he didn't understand all that was happening, appeared to be enjoying himself. The meeting ended after the usual prayers for special needs. I hoped that Bill would come forward for prayer, but he didn't. Instead, he came forward to say hello. "I told Gus about you," he told me, "and he wants to meet you."

That very night, after the prayer meeting, a crowd gathered in Larry and Paula's home for coffee and doughnuts. Again, there was much love and laughter and I got lost in the throng of people who filled the living room. When I finally sat down, I saw Bill standing alone at the entrance to the kitchen. He motioned to me and I followed him through the kitchen into the bedroom. Closing the door behind us, Bill sat down on the bed. As I moved to sit in the chair, I asked him how he enjoyed the meeting.

"I could listen to you talk all night," he replied. "You make people laugh. Religion wouldn't be so dull if we had more ministers like you. I know a lot of young people would want to listen to you talk about religion."

"Bill," I replied earnestly, "it's not a religion that I'm talking about; it's a personal relationship with Jesus Christ." He listened quietly and thoughtfully as I told him of Christ's redeeming love and the joy and victory that could be his in Jesus.

On that memorable night, Bill asked for and received Jesus into his heart. I was thrilled to be the witness of God's movement in Bill's life and immediately in his home. The Lord reestablished his relationships with his parents from whom he had been so distant. On the night of his conversion, Bill stayed up until three A.M. talking with his dad, something he had never done before. And, as a result of his conversion, Bill decided to stay at home with his family. His mother and sister noticed a sweetness about him that had not been there before. Having found new life in Jesus, as well as a new job and a car, Bill drew a beautiful picture of the Lord to celebrate his homecoming.

Never was a picture so deeply cherished by his family, for less than two weeks later, Bill and his friend, Gus, were killed in an automobile accident returning from a recording session. Bill had fallen asleep at the wheel.

Still, his family praises God even today, fully aware that their son was firmly established with them in Christ through God, the Father's gift of agape love. They were comforted by the Word of God, as Paul says in Philippians 1:21, "For to me to live is Christ and to die is gain... But I am hardpressed from both directions, having the desire to depart and be with Christ, for that is very much better..."

God's agape love had brought salvation to Bill and strength and praises to his family that will certainly join him, someday, in heaven.

AGAPE LOVE

DELIVERS FROM DELINQUENCY

While working among the poor of a small industrial town in New England, I was constantly surrounded by some of the toughest young derelicts imaginable. These were drug addicts, as well as alcoholic young people, some of them even brain-injured from using hard drugs. Others were slowly wasting away from the deadly deterioration process. All of these kids were what I called the down-and-outers. Some were so far out of the mainstream of life that they weren't even accepted in the drug culture! It was to these young people that I brought the healing message of forgiveness and salvation through Jesus Christ.

I had heard about Cindy long before I met her. She had a reputation for having sex with most of the boys in town. She was as loose with her morals as she was with the money from her welfare check. Cindy would buy beer and cigarettes for the boys or for anyone who dropped by her apartment. Her hangout was a large, dilapidated building on a main road that should have been declared uninhabitable. It was hard to determine which apartment was hers in this den of evil, for Cindy would periodically live-in with the various tenants. They were irresponsible young people without jobs who were living off the government.

The apartment building was not just Cindy's hangout. It was also the meeting place for most of the kids in the town who had nothing to do and no place to live. They usually went to the railroad tracks to drink and met at the park for their drugs. The apartment building was used for their sexual activity.

Venereal disease was rampant. Many of the teenagers, as well as an occasional married couple, would come to my office for help. Often, their most pressing needs seemed to be physical, but I usually had the opportunity to minister to their more important spiritual needs as well.

The sequence of places for those who wished to straighten out their lives was to the hospital for medical help, to the Salvation Army for physical help such as clothing and furniture, and finally to my office and prayer room for spiritual assistance. My office was within walking distance of the building where these teenagers met for their sex.

Cindy was twenty years old. She was married once, but was separated from her husband who was now living with another girl in Virginia. Mutual infidelity had destroyed their marriage after only a year. They had one child, and Cindy toted the infant around with her wherever she went. Most often, Cindy was seen with a twenty-four-year-old man named Dan, who was her likely counter-part.

Dan carried knives and boasted a brown belt in karate. He was quick to fight and occasionally served time for petty larceny or assault with a deadly weapon. Dan was well-known to the police department, with a police record a mile long in two states. He was also well-known to the young kids who idolized and feared him. The police left him alone as long as he would give them secret tips on the hard drug pushers. While I had seen Dan at a distance on the street, I had not as yet met him.

Meanwhile, the lost sheep slowly began to come to me because they knew that I was concerned about them. In answer to my prayers, God had placed His agape love in my heart for those who were abandoned by their families, their schools and their churches. Most of them came from broken homes. They desperately needed to hear that Jesus loved them and would forgive them of their sins if they would repent.

I had a refrigerator in the office with a supply of sandwiches and soda for anyone who was hungry. These were donated regularly by a supporter of the ministry. Undoubtedly, it was the food that brought some of those who came every day at noon one summer, but it didn't matter to me why they were coming. I saw their daily visits as a perfect opportunity to teach a Bible lesson. The office was replete with Bibles, tracts and magazines that were donated by different religious organizations. I found, however, that the attention span of these young people was not very long and that some of the teenagers couldn't even read. So, I used visual aids and stories from the children's Bible study book to reach them.

I listened to their gruesome accounts of the sex orgies and other activities in and out of the big house on the main road where Dan and Cindy were the unofficial rulers. Gradually, I won the confidence of a few of these kids who, in turn, genuinely reached out for help with their problems and found solutions in Jesus.

I extended my hand to the tortured souls that reached out for mine. Continually, I prayed;

"Dear heavenly Father, I ask You to give me Your perfect agape love for these wretched souls

91

that cry out for love and understanding. I pray that I might bring them Your comfort and Your compassion. Amen."

It was difficult for me to love these lost young people in a natural way. I was in prayer constantly. Their unwashed and diseased bodies were repulsive to behold. Of those who came barefoot, their lack of clothes coincided with their lack of understanding and acceptance by others. Sometimes, I would hug them against my will, believing that Jesus would have done the same.

The word was spreading throughout the area that I was a Jesus freak who was trying to convert everybody to religion. Many realized that I was reaching out to these fringe people when I began to look for a meeting place for them. City Hall knew that I cared about these kids, and through a newspaper article the general public learned that I was looking for a meeting house. But, there was little or no response from the people in the town. The general opinion was that these were degenerate kids who needed nothing more than a good strapping. I knew better, so I continued to search for what I thought was best for them.

As the needy kids came more and more often, I continued to give them comfort and healing through Jesus. Some received Him as Savior and their lives were transformed. These reborn young people, upon hearing and believing that Jesus cared about them, began to care about themselves by cleaning up and finding jobs. I helped them in any way I could.

As they filed in and out of my office, the dilapidated house on the main road that was once full of derelicts was now slowly emptying of its inhabitants. Dan and Cindy were infuriated as their kingdom of sexual servants began crumbling before their eyes. I became their public enemy number one. I began to receive abuse from them through their messengers. My name was a forbidden word in the building in which they lived. One young person came to me with the message, "Dan says that you better keep your nose out of his affairs. If you step foot in the building, you're a dead man." I returned the message, "Jesus loves you, Dan." Through another young person I had a New Testament sent to him. The following day, I found it torn to shreds on the floor in front of the office door. Beside the shriveled mess was a piece of paper with obscenities written on it. But, in the midst of this persecution, I prayed for the strength to persevere in finding a meeting place for the teenagers.

God answered that prayer through a young man who came to my office one day from another part of town. "I heard about the work you are doing with drug addicts," he told me. "I was a heroin addict for years until I gave my life to Jesus. God is leading me to help you find a coffee house for these needy kids."

I was thrilled. Together, we found a place and with the help of the kids themselves, we emptied my office of the hundreds of Christian books and pamphlets, as well as the furniture, that would help towards the humble beginnings of what we called the Christian Coffee House. The location was in the area of town where Dan and Cindy were still doing their own thing. It was an area that boasted of night people who frolicked in taverns and cafés. We thought it was an ideal setting, considering that the coffee house would bring light to the darkness.

The kids now had their own place to go, supervised by Christian adults. Occasionally, a band would come to play music in order to attract new young people. Many teenagers found their way in. God was moving, and I was grateful.

But, in the meantime, Dan and Cindy's hatred increased and they began to spread vicious rumors about me. I could tolerate the labels freak and fanatic, but I could hardly withstand the labels sex pervert and dope peddler. Actually, they accused me of the very things that they had been guilty of doing.

Things were changing too quickly for Cindy and Dan. Their followers were being converted to Christ and the old building in which they lived was almost empty. An intoxicated woman was injured as she fell on the broken stairs and now the town was finally declaring it unfit for habitation. With the prospects looking worse than ever for their immoral lifestyle, Dan and Cindy left the building, and then split up with one another after an argument. Cindy was refused her welfare checks soon after, so she took her baby and went to live with her mother in another section of town.

Meanwhile, Dan was on the warpath. He went to his probation officer and told him that I was corrupting the young people with drugs and sex. The probation officer believed him and stormed into my office one day demanding an accounting of the charge. Even though he refused to give me the name of my accuser, I knew that it was Dan. The probation officer waited defiantly for my reaction, but I didn't answer him. Jesus was my defense.

Although the officer could not prosecute me legally, he as much as told me to get out of town. As he continued to make other charges, eyeing me with suspicion and hatred, I prayed for God's agape love toward this officer beset with ignorance. In silence, I stood before this man with love in my heart. Flooded with God's peace, I watched him as he stormed out of my office. Then, I fell to my knees, thanking God for the strength to endure his charges and whatever followed.

I heard nothing more from the police about Dan's

allegations, so I remained on in the ministry to the troubled teenagers. But, although no evidence had established what Dan said as true, my reputation had been destroyed. I felt wounded and abandoned, wondering if my work was finished. Looking to the Scriptures for comfort, I read in the book of Proverbs, "To destroy another man's reputation is the same thing as plunging a sword into his body." Hurt deeply by the lies against my character, I then turned to the book of Romans where I read, "Bless those who persecute you; bless and do not curse them. Rejoice with those who rejoice, weep with those who weep."

I realized that God was showing me again that the only way I could bless Dan for what he'd done was through His agape love. My own love had failed once more. I asked God to transform the bitterness in my heart toward Dan and Cindy for the lies they had told about me.

God answered my prayer for agape love. Miraculously, as the days passed, I felt my bitterness turn to love and compassion for these poor, lost kids. God was preparing me for an unexpected meeting with Cindy.

Apologetically, a few days later, Cindy came to my office for help for the first and last time. She sat nervously in the chair explaining that welfare would no longer support her, and her mother had barely enough money for herself. Cindy desperately needed diapers and milk for the baby. She hadn't eaten herself in days. She cried with the remorse of Mary Magdalene as she confessed her guilt for the things that she had done. With my arms around her, and God's perfect love pouring down from heaven, Cindy prayed the sinner's prayer with me, her face buried in her hands. The following week, Cindy boarded a Greyhound bus with her baby and returned to her husband, looking forward to a new life.

And then, one day, I walked into my office and there

sat Dan looking as meek as a lamb and bearing a gift.

"I—well," he stammered, "I thought you might like to have this." He held out an antique Greek sword in a red velvet scabbard.

I must confess that I received the gift with apprehension, but I soon discovered that it was his way of saying that he was sorry for what he had done.

Dan sat on a chair, stonefaced and empty, head bowed, looking defeated. When he finally glanced up at me, I saw the misery in his eyes. I pulled my chair closer to his and began to tell him of Jesus' wonderful love and forgiveness, and of the new life waiting for him. With tears in his eyes, Dan asked God for forgiveness for his sins and asked Jesus to come into his heart with His cleansing love.

Today, Cindy and Dan, and many others whose lives were in a shambles, are new people because of Jesus and His perfect love. Cindy was reconciled with her husband and they are living happily in Virginia. Dan holds a steady job and enjoys hunting and fishing in his free time. And, all this was possible only through God's transforming agape love!

AGAPE LOVE

FREES FROM MENTAL ILLNESS

Jim was a forty-four-year-old clothing consultant from the suburbs of Chicago. When he was not traveling, he lived with his wife, Pat, and their six children who ranged in ages from five to thirteen. Slightly balding, Jim was an energetic and enterprising man who knew the clothing business well, particularly men's suits. He was a nominal churchgoer who boasted that two of his close friends were in the ministry.

I met Jim one summer on a flight from New York to Chicago. We were both in the front row of the no-smoking section of the plane. The cabin was full of people, except for a seat that separated us. Jim had placed his business folder on the empty seat as he began to read the New York Times. Dressed in a fashionable suit, he looked like a very successful businessman.

I was enroute to a publishing house near Chicago, dressed in my clerical garb. I paused, intermittently, while reading my Bible, to glance at the passenger beside me with the fancy cuff links.

Finally, he looked in my direction and asked cautiously, "Are you a clergyman?" When I answered yes, he asked rather abruptly, "Do you mind if I talk to you about a personal matter?"

"Not at all," I replied.

"My name is Jim," he began. "I go to church every Sunday, even though I don't understand the sermons. I have a wife and a family, and materially I have all that the world can offer. I'm successful in the clothing business and I make a substantial salary."

"What I'm about to tell you," he added, "I could never tell my pastor or his assistant even though both are my personal friends. It's easier to talk to you because I don't know you. Do you understand what I mean?"

"Yes, I do," I replied.

After a pause and a deep breath, Jim explained, "My wife has been in and out of psychiatric clinics for the past year. She had a nervous problem most of her life, but the last year has been very trying for me. Pat is constantly on medication and unable to take care of the kids and the housework properly."

After another pause, he plunged on, "I should be ashamed of what I've done, but I'm not. Yet, I do want your opinion anyway." Glumly, he continued, "I haven't had husband-wife relations with Pat more than twice during the past year. Last night, I had an affair with a woman I met in a hotel lobby. It never happened before and now, after it's over, I don't feel so bad about it."

Jim's confession was like a bomb dropping in our midst. He peered at me quizzically, evidently expecting an answer on the tip of my tongue. Never before had I heard such a startling admission delivered in such a casual manner.

My response was slow in coming. I explained to Jim that merely going to church on Sunday was not going to solve problems in or out of a home. I told him that a personal relationship with Jesus was the key to an understanding of the will of God as well as the forgiveness of our sins. I picked up the Bible on my lap and turned to the story of Nicodemus in the Gospel of John. Jim listened with interest as I read about being born again. Yet, while Jim appreciated my conversing with him, his all-important question remained unanswered—how can something be wrong when you don't feel bad about it?

My answer was that God has set down *His* guidelines for us to follow. I showed him in the Bible that it is not according to feelings that we are to follow the Lord's will, but in faith and obedience.

Jim admitted that he had never bothered to pray for Pat's healing. I assured him that God answers such prayer, citing the healings I had witnessed at various churches and prayer meetings throughout the country. Then, we prayed together in our seats for God's healing touch;

> *"Heavenly Father, we thank You for Your wonderful blessings of rebirth and forgiveness. I ask You to give Jim Your love and understanding; and to his beloved wife, Pat, Your healing, that she might be restored to a sound mind and body. I ask this in Jesus' name. Amen."*

Jim and I disembarked from the plane together. As we walked through the terminal, Jim, with suits over his shoulder and his folder under his arm, turned, and said, "I'm sure glad that I met you, because this whole thing with my wife has really been bugging me. Most of the guys at work," he added, "cheat on their wives often and they proclaim it publicly."

I reminded him that the ways of the world are not God's ways, and he agreed. Together, we picked up the rest of our luggage at the baggage area and then exchanged addresses. Almost as an afterthought, Jim asked, "Hey, Reverend, where are you going and how are you getting there?" When I told him that I was taking a limousine to a book publishing company, he suggested that I go in his car since the company was near his house.

I was amazed at how God provided for me that day. With time on my hands before a late afternoon appointment, I asked Jim to drop me off at the hotel so that I could get cleaned up. With a warm handshake and a hearty smile, Jim said good-bye and thanked me for helping him. I assured him that I was also blessed by our brief encounter.

My meeting at the publishing house was not very successful. As far as my plans with the publisher were concerned, my visit to Chicago was a dismal failure. I returned to my room at the hotel to spend the night. While I was musing over the day's events, the hotel operator buzzed to tell me that I had received a call while I was out. Wondering who it might be, I dialed the number she gave me. It was Jim. He said that both he and his wife would like to have me visit them and that he would come by the hotel to pick me up at eight-thirty.

Jim arrived just after I finished dinner. "You sure made a hit with my wife," he confided. "When I got home, I told her all about you and she and the kids want to meet you." While riding to the house, Jim added, "Pat doesn't often want visitors and she doesn't usually take to strangers. This *has* to be the beginning of a miracle. Do you think that God is beginning to answer my prayer?"

"I wouldn't be surprised at all," I answered.

"My oldest boy had heart surgery two years ago," Jim explained, "and we thought he wasn't going to live. He had to have a pacemaker inserted and he needed a blood transfusion. This really put a strain on us all, especially my wife. She's still fearful that Mike may not have a future. I guess fear is Pat's biggest problem. She is afraid for me, afraid for the children, and afraid for herself. She's in bad shape."

It had grown dark outside by the time we arrived at the house. As we entered the back door of Jim's suburban home, I could hear the pitter patter of children's feet and their playful voices in the basement. When Jim shouted, "We're here!" children seemed to come from every direction to meet the stranger. They gathered in a protective niche near the sofa where their mother sat.

The sight of giggling children distinctly offset the picture of a solemn-faced woman who looked at me with an empty stare as she said hello. The children were introduced one by one, and I smiled and shook hands with each of them. They all responded cheerfully, except the youngest, who withdrew his hand when I reached out. He went up to his mother and fearfully snuggled close to her side, his expression mirroring her own. It was as though he understood her plight.

All the children scattered at their father's command, except the youngest one, who had to be coaxed to leave his mother's side. Pat remained on the couch, nervously smoking her cigarettes, while Jim took me on a tour of their eight-room house. Their home was expensively furnished, but needed the hand of an enthusiastic housekeeper. Pat was too ill to take care of the house properly.

"Pat's hardest time is in the morning," Jim remarked. "She hasn't prepared breakfast in months. She has to gorge herself with medication to get through the day."

As we returned to the living room, Jim pointed out some artifacts he got from Spain while he was in the Navy. "I was really lost in the Navy," he recalled. "I'm glad I don't have to relive those sins again."

I walked across the living room and sat in a chair

directly opposite from where Pat sat, still nervously smoking. Jim sat down on the sofa beside his wife. The table next to the sofa was covered with cigarette ashes that overflowed from the ashtray and there were several vials of medication sitting in the midst of the ashes.

Pat was a pitiful sight to behold. It was apparent that she was doped up for it was all she could do to keep her eyes open. She spoke as though intoxicated.

"I'm so glad that you came to see me," she stammered. Tears began to trickle down her cheeks as she added, "I know that God has sent you to help me."

My heart leapt with the same agape love I had felt for the street urchins. Quietly, I answered her, "I love you, Pat, and Jesus loves you more than you will ever know."

"Do you really think so?" she asked wistfully. It was evident that she desperately needed the assurance that God had not abandoned her. Just then, Jim left the room to give Pat the privacy she needed to talk openly to me about her failings.

I moved across the room and sat in a straight-backed chair facing her. Reaching out to hold onto my hands, Pat blurted out all the painful things that were robbing her of the very healing she needed. In love, I assured her that Jesus would heal her that very night if she would just receive it. She was ecstatic just thinking of such a wonderful possibility.

With joy, Pat repeated these words after me;

"I thank You, Lord, for forgiving my sins. I stand now on the threshold of a new life and I ask You, Jesus, to come into my heart and to take over my life, that I might be set free from the bondage of sin forever. And, I ask You to heal my physical body as well as my spiritual one right now, in Jesus' name. Amen."

Pat lifted her head with a joyous smile on her face looking as though the clouds had parted forever in her life and the sun was now shining brilliantly upon her. "Jim— Jim," she shouted, "come quickly and bring all the children! I'm going to get better!"

Jim and the children ran into the living room to see what all the excitement was about. As the older children sat on the floor beside the sofa, Jim and the youngest one sat next to Pat. With a confidence that was as convincing as her smile, she said, "I feel so free! I feel so free! God is making me better. I feel better already!" Together, Pat and I praised God aloud in the midst of the startled spectators, "Praise You, Jesus, thank You, Jesus, praise You, Jesus, thank You, Jesus."

We all joined our hands and our hearts that evening in prayer and the Spirit of God came upon that whole household. We prayed as a family that Pat would claim her healing and her newly found freedom in Jesus. Together, we sang a song that I taught them called, "Amazing Grace." That night before I left, Pat threw her arms around me. I cried tears of joy because God had allowed me to be a witness of His mighty touch in another life.

That trip to Chicago was not in vain. My own plan was as dust, but God's plan provided a wonderful adventure in agape love.

Pat has received her healing from Jesus and now she meets the dawn of each day with praise on her lips and joy in her heart. She is finally the wife and mother that God wants her to be, healthy and alive in mind and body. Gone is all the medication she depended upon. And, gone forever from the life of her husband is the attitude that feelings are the guide to living. Today, Jim, too, walks gloriously by faith.

AGAPE LOVE

FORGIVES OUR ENEMIES

Dennis was a distinguished Christian lawyer from Massachusetts. A man in his early fifties, he had three children. I met him at a Christian retreat lodge in New Hampshire, and from time to time, we would travel together as a team in the ministry on the east coast.

Dennis' story of God's love begins in his childhood where he grew up in a devout Christian home. His father was the veritable partiarch of the family which included nine children. Dennis was the youngest in the family. He, like the other children, had a special devotion and respect for his kind and gentle father. In fact, Dennis idolized his father who was a lawyer and the head of his own law firm. His father encouraged him to be the best that he could possibly be, and Dennis wanted, more than anything else, to be like his dad.

Dennis' dad was a remarkable man. He embraced the legal practice, not only as a profession, but as a ministry. He had the kind of compassion and love that drew people to him. Many lives, fraught with misfortune and hardship, were transformed by the loving hand of Dennis' father who was eager to help others in spiritual and financial need. Church organizations experienced his generosity, as did almost everyone who came in contact with him.

His associates in the law firm knew better than anyone else that their boss was a man of compassion above and beyond the call of duty throughout a career that spanned almost four decades. Although Dennis' father was a man of outstanding caliber, he was very patient with the moral imperfections of his constituents. He became a private counselor to each of them in their problems, whether alcoholism, family difficulties or sickness.

As a courtroom lawyer, Dennis' dad was one of the best in the country. He practiced what he preached about working to reach the fullest of one's potential. He never hired men on the basis of religion or nationality; rather, he hired the man that could do the best job.

Although he was not pressured by his father, Dennis decided that he wanted to be a lawyer, too. His father guided him to a reputable law school and supported him with his encouragement and prayers. Dennis really had to plug to make it through, but he succeeded because of his tenacious will and the watchful eyes of his praying parents. Finally, Dennis passed his bar exams and was welcomed into his father's law firm.

Diligently, he set out to apply the theories he had learned at law school. His father was pleased to see the determination of his youngest son and the youngest member of the firm in handling difficult cases.

Now that he was in the office, Dennis carefully watched his father move about. He saw not only his method of handling difficult cases, but difficult people as well. Getting a first-hand view of his dad's generosity at the office, it began to really bother Dennis who was not inclined to be so unselfish.

His apprehension increased as he feared that his father was becoming a soft touch for people who would take advantage of him. He became even angrier at the steady stream of misfortunate people who would come by the office for a handout or a favor. Finally, Dennis could no longer contain his feelings. He confessed to his dad how he felt about the handouts, expressing his anger at seeing his father being "taken."

"Son," his dad quietly responded, "there is much joy in giving." He picked up his Bible from the desk and read, "It is more blessed to give than to receive." Then, turning a few well-worn pages, he read, "Inasmuch as ye have done it unto one of the least of these, my brethren, ye have done it unto Me."

Setting his Bible down, his dad continued, "When I am in a position to help another, either spiritually or financially, I am actually doing it for the Master. If you were to see the joy in the faces of the people I have helped; if you were to know how lives have been changed for the better spiritually because of financial help, you would change your attitude."

However, Dennis remained unconvinced.

The years passed quickly. Dennis had made a name for himself in the law practice throughout New England. It was finally time for him to take over the firm and for his dad to retire after a long and successful career. Dennis was ready for the job after having been seasoned by years of experience and wisdom.

As the new head of the firm, Dennis continued in his father's traditions. Except for the handouts for the needy, Dennis carried on all of his father's successful policies. Thus, the company expanded and new partners were added.

Then, one day, Dennis audited the books of the firm himself in order to ascertain payroll percentages for employees. This was something his father had done rarely. To his horror, Dennis discovered that Max, one of the oldest members of the firm, who was in charge of the books, had padded his expense account for a period of twenty years. He had stolen literally thousands of dollars from the firm.

Dennis was shocked, for he knew that this was a man for whom his father had made many allowances and sacrifices over the years. Max had a drinking problem and Dennis' father had given him time off with pay on countless occasions during his career. Max's sin of theft was not merely a sin against justice or a sin against the firm. Worst of all, Dennis thought, it was a sin against his own father who had made sacrifices for Max that were beyond reason.

According to the law, Max could be prosecuted for this crime that would warrant his serving many years in prison. Dennis would be justified in having this thief seized by the police and dealt with accordingly. However, he did not want to tell his father about the betrayal of a so-called friend. It would deeply hurt his dad who was now in ill health. Besides, Dennis did not want to disgrace the family name by divulging such a terrible crime against the legal profession.

Instead, Dennis prosecuted Max in his own way. With all the hatred and vengeance that a human spirit could possess, he confronted Max with his crime, and then banished him from the distinguished law firm forever. Dennis could have literally killed Max for what he had done to his father.

In the months that followed, Dennis was still extremely upset at the thought that the firm was not totally compensated for the crime that Max committed. As a result, a deep resentment continued to grow in his heart.

A short time later, Dennis' father lay dying as a result of a stroke. His family gathered prayerfully around his bedside. All were Christians, except Dennis, whose stubborn will had separated him from God.

Love was the force that finally broke Dennis' shell. As his dear father lay on his deathbed, Dennis was moved by his sister to accept Jesus as his Lord and Savior. With a smile and a handclasp from his dad, who had prayed so long for his conversion, Dennis tearfully made his peace with God on his knees beside his father's bed. A new Christian was born as another went to his heavenly home. Though this was a day of sadness, it was also a day of rejoicing. Dennis had placed his life in the hands of Jesus Christ.

Soon after, Dennis returned to the law firm a new Christian. Those who worked with him remarked that he was becoming a pleasant co-worker instead of a demanding taskmaster. They wondered what had happened to him. But, Dennis knew only too well that it was Jesus changing his life from deep within.

As he read his father's Bible with great interest, he was delightfully amazed that wherever he turned, there was a Scripture passage about becoming a new creature. God was showing him that he had to put off the old things and former ways if he wished to be as Christ wanted him. Formerly, Dennis was arrogant and curt, but now he was becoming gentle and loving with his family and with people on the job. And, he was learning how to take his problems to the Lord.

Formerly, Dennis had a driving spirit. His work came first and he would burn the midnight oil beyond reason just to win a legal battle. Now, his relentless efforts resulted in a mild heart attack. The Lord taught Dennis that he didn't have to try so hard to do things in his own strength. Finally, he realized that he had to trust God more than he trusted himself.

Dennis had always been the first to complain when his father would give money away to needy causes like "Santa Claus." Then, the Lord's searchlight, the Bible, revealed this fault to him, also, that he might correct it. Gradually, Dennis did become as generous as his dad. The Lord had done a wonderful job changing a life according to *His* pattern.

A new ministry began to unfold in the law firm. Tracts and Bibles were seen throughout the office. Dennis attended Christian conferences enthusiastically to learn the scriptures, that he might become the measure of the man Christ wanted him to be.

As the years passed, the task of rooting out the old and bringing in the new continued. Spiritually, Dennis grew on to maturity. Yet, there was an unresolved area in his life that needed to be dealt with. It was his hatred and resentment towards Max. The slightest thought of this man produced sleepless nights for Dennis who needed all the sleep he could get in order to carry on his work both as a lawyer and as a Christian. But, there was no rest from the memory of this scoundrel, Max. Dennis wanted to continue walking in the blessings of the Lord, but if that blessing had anything to do with Max, he wanted no part of it.

As the light of God's Word continued to shine in dark corners, Dennis finally admitted what had to be done. He needed to surrender this hatred for Max that prevented him from further blessings in the Lord. So, one night, Dennis prayed, "Dear Lord, I'm sorry for this resentment I have toward Max, but he did a pretty disgusting thing to dad after dad was so good to him."

"You must surrender this resentment to me," the Lord answered, *"and ask for healing in this situation."* In submission, Dennis prayed for release from the hatred toward Max and for the healing. Then, the Lord spoke to him again with one more instruction, *"I want you to go to Max, personally, and ask him to forgive you for the hatred you have felt toward him all these years."*

"I can't do that, Lord!" Dennis returned sharply. "Max will think I'm a fool. Besides, he's the one who committed the sin, not I."

Then, the scripture passage was quickened to him, "For all have sinned and fallen short of the glory of God." Suddenly, Dennis realized that he was responsible before God for his own sins of hatred and resentment, regardless of what Max had done.

Even then, only a miracle could possibly see Dennis through such a seemingly impossible request from the Lord. He just could not ask Max for forgiveness in his own strength. The healing of his heart that Dennis had prayed for had not yet come. There was one prayer, however, that could perform the miracle of giving him the ability to face Max with God's love. Realizing he had no love of his own for Max, Dennis asked the Lord for *His* agape love.

He prayed;

"Dear heavenly Father, thank You for Your light that shows me the darkness in my life. I ask You to place in me Your love for Max who stole thousands of dollars from my dad. I need Your love, Father, that the sin of resentment may be healed forever in my heart. I ask this in Jesus' name. I want to be free from this bondage of hatred and unforgiveness. Amen."

Over the years, Max had moved to another part of town, where he still practiced law. Twice, Dennis went to Max's office building, but didn't have the courage to face him in order to ask for his forgiveness. Finally, on the third try, standing firm on the faith of that prayer for agape love, Dennis took the elevator to the ninth floor of the office building.

Nervously, he knocked on the door and a receptionist appeared. He asked for Max and was seated in the office waiting room. Max was with a client, so Dennis had to wait for fifteen minutes to see him. It was the longest wait in his life.

When the client left, Dennis was directed into Max's office. As their eyes met, they both froze. Max's mouth dropped in surprise as he exclaimed, "Dennis, what are you doing here?"

"Max," Dennis replied, measuring his words carefully, "I've hated you all these years for what you did to my father by stealing that money. I actually wanted to kill you for it."

"Dennis, you were good to me. You could have had me sent to jail."

"God has placed His love in my heart for you, Max," Dennis continued resolutely, "and I've come here today to ask you to forgive me for the hatred that I've felt for you all these years."

Max's face flushed red as tears sprang to his eyes. "No, Dennis," he said brokenly, "I shouldn't be forgiving *you*, I need to be forgiven *by you*." Tears poured down the two men's faces as they embraced each other with God's love surrounding them.

The healing and blessing that came to Dennis was overwhelming as he left Max's office that day. He never felt so light and free. And, blessings continue to surround Dennis today because he has learned the marvelous lesson of how God's agape love takes over in our weakness, teaching us the kind of forgiveness that Jesus displayed on the cross.

AGAPE LOVE

BLESSES CHILDREN

It was a hot day in August. I had flown to Miami, Florida, for a funeral and afterwards I was invited to stay in Fort Lauderdale at the home of Sid and Laurie. They were a radiant Christian couple, relatives of the deceased.

After breakfast, we sat around the dining room table for scripture study and sharing. It was a blessed time of discussion in the presence of the Holy Spirit, as our attention was repeatedly drawn to the love section in first Corinthians, chapter thirteen. Each of us agreed that love best summed up the challenge facing Christians everywhere. Sid, Laurie and I admitted that our biggest failures had been with love. Also, we agreed that our efforts to do good for others were always in vain if they were not accompanied by love.

We were rather lost in our conversation, when our train of thought was interrupted by a gentle knock on the door. Laurie and Sid called, "Come in," and in walked Doris, a vivacious white-haired Christian friend in her late fifties. Trailing behind her was her five-year-old grandson, Stan, who stomped in with giant steps. He looked as normal as any other child his age, cute and full of activity.

I was introduced to Doris who was really excited about meeting another Christian from out of state. "I'm really happy to be here today to meet you," she said. "Between my job and babysitting my little grandson, I rarely get out for fellowship." She noticed the open Bibles and asked, "May I join you in your Bible study?" Enthusiastically, Doris sat down at the table and opened her well-worn Bible, and together we resumed our discussion on love.

Meanwhile, little Stan was running around the house imitating the sounds of an Indian warrior. I pretended not to notice the harsh noises that he was making while running like a madman, and we continued reading from first Corinthians. Sid was reading aloud, "Love is patient, love is kind, love does not envy, love is not pretentious, love is not puffed up," when we heard a loud thud in the hallway outside the bedroom. It shook the whole house. It sounded like a pipe breaking in the cellar to me, but it turned out to be Stan, throwing himself off a chair. Doris rebuked him and warned him that he would not get a hamburger that day if he didn't stop misbehaving. He listened, smirking, and then continued to run around the house.

"Stan has a lot of energy for a five-year-old," I remarked.

"Oh, please don't let Stan bother you," Doris replied. "He has a lot to get out of his system. He doesn't have a father and his mother is no better. She runs around with anyone she can find." Doris began to cry as Laurie grabbed her hand. Tears streamed down her cheeks as she sobbed uncontrollably over the condition of her only child, Stan's mother.

"I've prayed so many times to God, asking Him to do something for my daughter and her son," Doris sobbed. "I just can't go on like this. It's too much pressure for me to carry this horrible burden. Where did I go wrong?"

Softly, Laurie comforted Doris, "Don't worry, dear, we love you and we know that God will take care of the whole situation. Just continue to give the burden to Him and He will uphold you."

Then, we all joined hands to pray;

"Heavenly Father, Author of all love, we come to You in this need. We ask You to lift this burden from Doris. We ask You to comfort her with Your love. We know that You are sovereign in every situation. Take this whole situation, heavenly Father, and change it for Your glory. We claim the lives of Doris's daughter and her grandson, Stan. Make Your love real to them. And, may we continue to dwell in Your love. We ask this in Jesus' name. Amen."

After we prayed, I suggested that we resume our sharing on love. But, there was no way that we could continue with Stan running about the house. At that moment, God spoke directly to my heart. He said to me, *"You Christians can talk up a blue storm about love. But,"* the Lord chided, *"how can you continue sharing about love when little Stan is starving for My love? Do you think that he is going to receive it by osmosis? Go ahead. Go love that little boy with My love."*

I had never received such a clear commission from the Lord before. I rose from the table and my three companions seemed to know immediately what I had to do. They began to pray silently as I went to look for Stan to love him with God's love. With that special love in my heart, I reached down to pick him up. I sat down on the living room couch and took him on my knee. Quietly, I said, "Stan, I love you and Jesus loves you."

Suddenly, his face contorted, changing from indifference to a vile hatred. "I hate you!" he cried emphatically. He kicked me on the knee while pushing and scratching to get away. Spitting at me, he ran into the bedroom.

I was stunned at his behavior. My "so-called" love was immediately changed to anger. My thoughts were racing. "God is dealing with me in a way like never before," I realized. I was being tested on all my beliefs in agape love, and it looked like I was failing miserably.

Frustrated, I muttered to myself, "I am justified to spank that fresh kid for what he just did to me. I know that if I had carried on in the presence of adults like that as a child, I would have received a severe spanking."

But, God was saying otherwise, *"No, you must love this little boy with My love, not yours."*

I realized that I did not have the kind of love in myself that this situation called for, so I began to cry out to God, *"Dear Lord, put Your love for Stan in me. I can't possibly love a child like him on my own."*

With that prayer finished, I resolutely followed Stan into the bedroom. He was sitting on the floor beside the bed. Lying down beside him, I offered another quick, silent prayer. Then, I repeated the words the Holy Spirit had given me, "I love you, Stan. And, Jesus loves you."

"I hate you! I hate you!" he screamed with all his might. His voice did not seem to be his own. With this exclamation of hate, there followed a barrage of dirty words which spewed out of his mouth like vomit.

As he shouted epithets that only a grownup would understand, I began to sense the gravity of this struggle within myself between the flesh and the spirit. My flesh wanted to lash out at this "little monster," but the spirit within me wanted to love him. Beads of sweat poured off my forehead as I resisted my impulse to retaliate in anger and instead returned love for his hatred. Again, I said,

"Jesus loves you, Stan, and I love you." As I remained in a prone position on the bed, Stan grabbed a hair brush from the dresser and threw it at me, hitting my shoulder. The tension mounted as I muttered wearily, "I love you, and Jesus loves you." Suddenly, Stan jumped on top of me and started pounding on my back as though on bongo drums. He pounded while shouting obscenities, as though he desperately needed to be emptied of a deep reservoir of hatred that had been within him for a long, long time.

The struggle inside me was almost unbearable and I was aware at that point that it was not a battle against flesh and blood, but rather against principalities and powers as the Bible says in the book of Ephesians, chapter six.

Again, I shouted resolutely, "Jesus loves you, and I love you!" Surprisingly, Stan appeared to be suddenly exhausted from all the pounding. Once again, he sat on the floor beside the bed. There was a moment of silence while I waited for the next obscenity. But, instead, Stan murmured, "Will you play with me?" I could hardly believe my ears. I thought they were playing tricks on me. "Why do you want me to play with you?" I asked him. "Do you love me?"

"Yes," he returned sharply, "I do love you." Then, abruptly, he checked himself, "No, I don't love you! I hate you!" His voice had changed again and sounded harsh and severe, like that of an angry adult.

Just then, Doris called to him from the kitchen, "Come, Stanley, it's time to go." Little Stan ran out of the bedroom as fast as he could, shouting, "I hate you, I hate you, I hate you!"

"Joe is leaving tomorrow. Say good-bye, Stan," suggested his grandmother. Instead, Stan flung the door wide open and ran out to the car. Doris apologized for the way that her grandson had acted that day, but I assured her that it was all right. Then, as Laurie and Sid were saying good-bye to Doris, I quietly went out to the car to say good-bye to Stan. He was so ruffled and angry that he could not close the front car window in order to shut me out.

Again, I spoke the words that the Spirit had given me, "I love you, Stan, and Jesus loves you." With one final effort, Stan screamed furiously at me, burying his face in his hands so that he wouldn't even have to look at me. At that moment, Doris walked outside and got into the car, noticeably upset at the behavior of her grandson. She asked him, once more, if he wanted to say good-bye, but Stan retaliated with, "I hate him!"

Doris was deeply embarrassed for me and for herself. "I'm really amazed at Stan's behavior," she apologized. "It's never been this bad before. I hope that our next visit will be more pleasant."

Discouraged, I watched the car speed away before returning to the house. The hurt expressions on Sid and Laurie's faces only faintly echoed the sorrow that I felt within.

Laurie spoke with compassion, "We know what you were trying to do, Joe, and we were praying that you would succeed. But, God doesn't work that way, does He?"

"Maybe it takes more time," I replied wearily, "but I really hoped that things would turn out better than they did."

"You look tired, Joe," Sid interjected. "Why don't you go lie down and rest?" He was right. I was the victim of spiritual exhaustion. I went into the bedroom totally worn out, but I couldn't sleep.

Within an hour, the phone rang and Laurie called me

from the kitchen. I stumbled out of the bedroom as she handed me the receiver. It was Doris, excited and jubilant. I could hear her crying tears of joy as she exclaimed, "Oh, Joe, I'm so happy. I don't know how to tell you this, but something has happened to Stan. He's different! While I was driving home he started crying uncontrollably and he looked awfully pale. I thought I would have to take him to the doctor. I asked him what was wrong and he answered, 'I love him, but I hate him.' I knew he was talking about you, Joe. He vomited in the car. Now, he is sitting in a chair, peaceful and quiet. I have never seen him this way before. Oh, Joe, I'm so happy I can't keep from crying. Stan wants to talk to you himself."

Doris gave the phone to Stan. What heavenly joy it was to hear words of love from this little boy.

"Joe, I love you," he whispered.

"And, do you love Jesus?" I asked him.

"Yes," he replied.

Stan had begun to sound like the little boy God intended him to be. "Joe," he asked then, "will you stay for one more day so that I can see you?"

"Yes," I replied, overjoyed.

Doris took the phone and assured me that both she and Stan would like to return on the following morning to thank God for this answer to prayer. After hanging up the phone, Sid, Laurie, and I began to thank God ourselves for showing us that love truly is the most important ministry.

"Thank You, Jesus," I began to pray, "for showing me that even through the most harrowing experiences, Your love wins out when we ask You for it."

At nine A.M. the next morning, Doris and Stan arrived. Expectantly, I flung open the front door. Doris was beaming from ear to ear as Stan threw his arms around

127

me when I bent down and reached out for him. He squeezed me tightly in a genuine expression of love. Then, as we all watched, Stan took Laurie by the hand and pulled her into the bedroom, motioning her to sit down on the bed. Jumping up on the bed himself, he hugged her as he had never done before. Later, Laurie remarked that it was as though God Himself were loving her through this little boy. Because of the gift of agape love shown to him, Stan was now able to *give* love as well as *receive* it. His embrace of Laurie was his way of saying thank you to all of us for loving him for so long with God's love.

That morning, Stan received Jesus into his heart. And, Jesus received Stan in much the same way as He did other little ones, two thousand years ago, when He said, "Suffer little children, and forbid them not, to come unto me; for of such is the kingdom of heaven."

The five of us praised God with hands raised in the living room that day. Yes, even little Stan joined us in our praises. And, it was through the miraculous change in Stan that his mother subsequently consecrated her life to God!

How wonderfully our God answers prayer! Now, Laurie, Sid, Doris, her daughter, Stanley, and I have a beautiful story to share with everyone about the power of God's perfect agape love.

AGAPE LOVE

CURES THE INCURABLE

More than a year ago, I gave a talk about healing at a women's Bible study in Rhode Island. After the session, I was heading for my car in the parking lot when a middle-aged woman named Minnie stopped me and told me about her mother. "I know you are a busy person," she said, "but my mother is dying of cancer and I wonder if you might have some idea of what we can do for her. Maybe you have some insight about healing that would help her. This might sound far-fetched," she added, hurriedly, "but may I give you my phone number and address just in case you feel led to call or write to me? My mother is in a hospital in North Carolina."

I told the eager woman that I would do what I could. My address book was filled with names and addresses of people from all over the country. I thought, "One more name couldn't hurt any."

Later, as I was preparing for a trip overseas, I was in my hotel room at the airport in New York, catching up on correspondence, when it occurred to me that I had not called this devout Christian woman. I hadn't received a special word for her mother as I scanned my address book, either.

Because of snow, my flight overseas was postponed. While in prayer, as I lingered at the airport another day, it dawned on me that I should visit Minnie's sick mother in person. It would not slow down my schedule any more than the snow had already done.

So, I phoned Minnie, telling her that I would be glad to visit her mother in North Carolina and to pray for her healing. She was amazed and overjoyed, never expecting this response from me. She told me that both her dad and her sister lived close to the hospital, and she assured me that one of them would pick me up at the airport in North Carolina and provide for my lodging.

I hung up the phone, and not knowing what lay ahead of me, I prayed;

"Dear Lord, You have led me thus far and this trip seems to be a leap into the blue. Give me the confidence to persevere on this mission and not to fear whatever obstacles may be on my path. Give me the faith to pray for this healing, and may it be a complete healing in every way."

Having scheduled the flight, I packed my bags and boarded the plane for the South. I was greeted at the airport by Minnie's sister, Charlotte, an attractive woman in her late thirties.

"I'm so grateful you came," she said. "Mother is just thrilled, knowing you're coming to see her. Perhaps we can go straight to the hospital after we take your bags to the house. Minnie and I have much faith in God's power, but mother seems to have lost her faith through the ordeal of her sickness."

As we drove to the house, Charlotte told me that her husband, Alan, was not in agreement with her in spiritual matters. "Alan thinks religion is a lot of nonsense," she warned me. "I doubt if he will appreciate your being here. He is a very skeptical person by nature."

Already it appeared that I was going to need special

grace from God to perform this mission successfully. But, wanting to strengthen Charlotte's faith, I said confidently, "Let's trust God to take care of the loose ends. I genuinely felt led to come here, and your mother is the person that I came to help."

When we were still a few miles from her house, Charlotte said, "I know that your intentions are the best and I think I understand the faith that operates in your life. It seems to be an unusual ministry that you have. I just hope my husband won't be rude to you after all your efforts in coming here."

We arrived at Charlotte and Alan's suburban home and their three children met us at the door. Then, Alan appeared. He looked tense as he greeted me and shook my hand. I felt an atmosphere of gloom surround us as Alan interrogated me in the living room, with my bags not yet unpacked. He asked me questions about my background, my education, and my motivation for coming. The three children were sitting on the floor like jurors in a courtroom as they listened to my responses. I managed to remain deliberate and optimistic in the face of the apparent suspicion from this man who simply could not understand.

I was shown to a room and immediately began to unpack. A few minutes later, I heard Charlotte and Alan exchange tense words with one another, arguing about whether I should visit the hospital that very evening or wait until the following day. Charlotte was convinced that her mother was waiting expectantly with her father for my arrival, and that it was too early for her to be asleep.

Charlotte drove to the hospital because Alan did not want to go, preferring to stay at home with the children. While on the way, Charlotte made no mention of Alan. The conversation centered upon her mother instead.

"Mother is so happy that you're coming," Charlotte confided again. "The doctors say she has terminal cancer. She is heavily sedated, and isn't responding to the chemotherapy. What concerns me most is that her spirit is deeply troubled. She's bitter toward God because she feels that He is punishing her. My sister, Minnie, has come to visit Mother several times during her illness, attempting to communicate joy and faith to her, but we don't see too much response. Father is suffering terribly and he feels so helpless. I'm sure that he'll be glad to see you, too."

As we arrived at the hospital parking lot, I asked Charlotte the question that had been uppermost in my mind. "Tell me, Charlotte, has your mother committed her whole life to Christ?"

"Mother has always been a good woman," she replied, "although she has never been a churchgoer. She has carried a bitterness in her heart toward God for years because of the fire that ravished the home of her parents, killing both of them in their retirement years. Mother has never understood why her beautiful Christian mother would have been taken in such a horrible way."

As we rode the elevator, I felt my pulse quicken. So I prayed;

"Dear God, this is a big task. My faith is small. Give me the confidence to walk strong in this hour. I don't feel that the welcome mat is out for me. Yet, I know that You can accomplish Your perfect will in spite of the circumstances. Give me Your agape love for these people. Prepare this mother's heart that there might be a response to Your Holy Spirit. I pray in Jesus' name. Amen."

Charlotte's father, a kindly, white-haired man, was standing just outside the hospital room. We shook hands

134

as he said, "I sure appreciate your coming all this way to see my wife, Valerie. She's awake, now, and I know she'll be happy to see you."

As I entered the room, Valerie looked up, realizing that I must be her expected visitor. "Oh, thank you for coming," she exclaimed. "My daughter, Minnie, told me all about you." I greeted her with a kiss as she lay curled up as though in pain. Her husband stood at the foot of the bed, Charlotte at one side, and me at the other.

Looking back and forth at each of us, Valerie began to cry, "Why is God doing this to me? The pain is so strong that I just want to die."

Her husband started to cry then, and Charlotte began to pray quietly. Taking Valerie's hand in mine, I asked her if she had ever surrendered her life to Christ.

"I believe in Jesus," she sobbed, "and I don't think I've ever gone against Him. I've tried to do the best I could as a wife and mother."

After explaining the details of God's plan of salvation through Jesus' death and resurrection to her, I reassured Valerie that God was not punishing her as she seemed to think, but that He would bless her in new and wonderful ways if she would totally commit her life to Christ.

Eagerly, Valerie repeated these words after me;

"Dear Lord Jesus, I come to You as a sinner, but knowing that You died and rose again that my sins would be forgiven. I confess those sins to You now, Jesus, and ask You to come into my heart with Your cleansing love. I commit my entire life to You, Lord, from this day forth. In Jesus' name. Amen."

Before we prayed for her healing, I asked Valerie if she had any resentments toward any of her family or friends or toward God. She admitted that she had and the tears began to flow again as she surrendered her resentments, too. Then, together, the four of us asked the Lord for her healing.

As we joined hands around her bed, I began to softly praise God. After a few minutes of silence, we all raised our voices in a song of praise. Valerie joined us, her eyes reflecting her newfound peace and joy. As I stood beside her bed, I had an assurance that this was the reason for which I had come and that having witnessed Valerie's surrender to Christ, my purpose had been accomplished. But, Valerie asked if I would stay a few more days for she wanted me to visit her again in the hospital. I promised her I would, and then we all said good night so that Charlotte and I could return home.

The children were asleep when we arrived, and Alan was reading *The Wall Street Journal* in the living room. Looking up, he asked how the hospital visit went. Charlotte and I said fine, nearly in unison, but Charlotte said nothing about what had actually happened. Sensing the tension between them, I remained quiet, also. Alan did not understand my reason for coming and he couldn't help but communicate his suspicions by his words and attitude.

"Don't you think you are building up false hopes in my mother-in-law by coming here?" he asked me, frowning intently. "If she is meant to die, why are you trying to go against what the doctors are saying? Religion at this point could be destructive."

Quietly, I answered him, "Though one lives, or dies, I believe that both can be done in the peace of Christ. And, everyone can know that perfect peace. Also, I have seen people miraculously healed of many diseases," I continued. "I am motivated by my faith which has been strengthened through the witness of countless miracles in my own life and in the lives of others."

Alan remained unconvinced. "I believe in reality, not fantasy. Are there others who think the way you do?"

I assured him of the growing number of Christians who were seeing God's wonderful signs in these days. Then, I shared my own testimony of my conversion to Christ. But, Alan was only more convinced than ever that I was out on a limb and he began to ask me what my credentials were. Willingly, I gave him the information about my educational background, but because it would do more damage than good, I withheld the fact that I had barely enough money to get overseas and back.

After retiring that evening, I felt like a stranger in a foreign country. Lying in bed, I could think of a hundred other places that I would rather be, but I knew that there was some divine purpose in my being *exactly* where I was.

On the following day, I went back to the hospital to see Valerie. Again, she told me how grateful she was that I had come so far to visit her. Eagerly, she confided that she wanted to know what it was to wake up in the morning with joy and peace in her heart. She wanted to know how to greet the birds with a song like her daughter, Charlotte, did. In essence, Valerie wanted to know how to live a victorious life.

I told her about praise, explaining that when we praise God it lifts our spirits and brings us into His very presence, where He blesses us. I shared the scripture in Psalm two which says that God *inhabits* the praises of His people, meaning that He dwells there, and that our praise is holy and acceptable in His sight.

Together, Valerie and I prayed a psalm of praise. Valerie had to learn, as most of us do, that the simplest words of love and praise are the most pleasing in the sight of God. It was during this second visit that Valerie's hands were raised in praise to her Savior.

Just before going overseas, I contacted the prayer community in Valerie's area to pray for her complete healing. When I returned to the States sometime later, I immediately phoned Minnie and heard the glorious news of the miracle that had taken place. Valerie had been totally healed of the cancer! She was up and walking about, well in spirit, soul, and body, and eagerly looking forward to teaching arts and crafts to underprivileged children.

Today, Alan remains unconvinced, but his wife and sister-in-law have been strengthened in their faith and commitment to Jesus Christ. People don't always believe when they see miracles, but they *do* see miracles when they believe! We pray for further miracles to be brought to that family through God's wondrous agape love.

AGAPE LOVE

GIVES PURPOSE TO LIFE

While on a visit to Washington, D.C., a few years ago, I met a young Russian naval officer who told me the story of how a girl's love brought him to the foot of the cross.

His name was Sergei. When you met him, you had the impression that you were meeting a Goliath from the Old Testament for he stood well over six feet tall and his hands were massive. He had an intensity about his mission, as though there were a great pressure upon him to share his convictions. I found him distinctly impressive in every way.

I met with Sergei in a Christian home in Maryland. On the previous day he was at a church where he had given his testimony of receiving Christ as his Savior. Now, in an informal gathering with three others, he repeated the highlights of his escape to freedom.

Sergei grew up as an orphan in Russia. Never knowing the love of a mother or father, he curried the favor of his teachers and welcomed their appreciation for his hard work and his brilliant achievements. Sergei vividly recalled the many orphanages he had attended, and the boys like himself who were without the warmth of a home and a family. Through it all, he developed a compassion for his classmates, as well as a driving spirit to achieve.

Sergei was a superior student, not only in academics,

but also in athletics. As a teenager, he was chosen one of the most excellent youths in Russia having excelled in almost every conceiveable area of physical and intellectual development. As a result, he was given one of the highest awards ever received by a Russian youth.

Sergei was taught from his earliest years that Russia held the only key to absolute power and freedom. Religion, he was taught, was for weak men. He was thoroughly ingrained to believe that the Russian government was telling the truth about life, about freedom—and about God.

Demonstrating his leadership potential among his fellow students, Sergei was selected by the Russian government to be the head of the Russian Youth Police. It was the job of the Youth Police to make raids upon religious meetings. Whether these meetings were held in homes, underground churches, or meeting halls, the Youth Police operated efficiently in the execution of its task, inflicting violence upon ministers, priests, and people who held clandestine meetings in opposition to the rules of the Soviet government. Religious assemblies were banned and opposition to these rules was dealt with harshly.

As Sergei later related, he was only following orders when he frequently took part in the brutal torture and evacuation of these "fanatical" people who defied the government. Disobedience to the Soviet government was a capital sin and the punishment was made to fit the crime. Those who met secretly to worship their Jesus were (and still are) regarded by the government of the Soviet Union as dissidents. Bloodshed, broken bones and bruised bodies were the normal occurence when Sergei made his raids with the Youth Police.

One day, while on a typical raid in the basement of a building, Sergei and his hatchet men beat up a group of Christians who were meeting for prayer and Bible study. A young girl of about fifteen with a beautiful, innocent face was among them. She was pushed around by Sergei and his young cohorts who bruised her with their clubs just as they did the others. As the Christians were being evacuated from the meeting, Sergei warned all of them that they would pay a far greater price for their disobedience if they were ever caught again.

A short time later, Sergei and his Youth Police saw the young girl, not quite recovered from her past wounds, at another clandestine meeting. She had not heeded their warning. When she was discovered, she was thrown on a table and clubbed unmercifully. Sergei vividly recalled how, even as she experienced excruciating pain, she lay there with love in her eyes. Looking directly at him, her glowing face seemed to speak freely of Jesus' forgiveness.

Bewildered, Sergei could not understand what inspired love and forgiveness in a girl that had nearly died a martyr's death. He had persecuted and even killed other Christian dissenters, yet never had he seen such peace as in that girl's eyes; never before had he witnessed this godly love that could renew life so close to the point of death. As questions continued to whirl through Sergei's mind, he began to search for the answers.

It was not long afterwards that Sergei finished his term in the Youth Police and joined the Russian Naval Fleet. While on a huge vessel in the Pacific Ocean off the coast of British Columbia, he grew disenchanted and restless. He could not sleep at night. In his bunk he would toss and turn, remembering the face of the young Christian girl whom he had nearly murdered. Her beautiful face and determination to serve her God haunted him continually. It was at this point in his life that Sergei's feelings toward Russia began to change.

"Russia has lied to me," he thought. "I have been obedient to her wishes and still I am not free. I have been her victim.

"These Christians must have true freedom. I have seen this freedom in the face of the girl who appears to me at night in my dreams. There must be something true about the Christian message. It seems to uplift the spirits of those who profess it. Who is this Jesus for whom these Christians are willing to die?"

Risking his own life, but more anxious to find the freedom he was looking for away from Russian shores, Sergei plunged into the icy waters of the Pacific. He swam feverishly away from the Russian vessel until it became a speck on the horizon. Sergei had done what few had ever lived to talk about; he had defected from Russia. His excellent physical condition helped him to survive the cold and the cramps as long as he did. He continued to swim for hours beyond his own strength until he finally lost consciousness, somehow managing to drift in the choppy waters with his arms draped over large pieces of rubble.

Sergei miraculously managed to regain consciousness long enough to make it to the Canadian shore where he was soon discovered. Unconscious, he was brought to a Canadian hospital where he lay for many days, oblivious to his surroundings. As he regained consciousness, having been nursed back gradually by the medical staff, Sergei explained his identity to the Canadian police. He told them that he had defected from Russia; that he would rather die than go back. Immediately, the Canadian police checked his story and discovered that he was telling the truth. Soon after, he was visited by officials from the Russian embassy in Canada who severely admonished him to return to Russia. But, Sergei told them that he could not return to a government which lied to its people and kept them in slavery through force and deception.

Finally, a small group of sympathetic Christians took him under their wing. Not long afterwards, Sergei knelt in the sancturary of a small country church, surrounded by a group of witnesses, and committed his life to Jesus Christ, asking and receiving forgiveness for his many sins of violence and desecration against the Christians he had persecuted in Russia. Now, Sergei began to understand the freedom and the love that he had seen in the face of the young girl who had nearly died a martyr's death at his hand. The community of those with whom he was worshiping were his true friends and he had come to love them.

As he grew spiritually, Sergei had a driving desire to share with others, especially young people, how Jesus can replace hatred with love and fear with peace. Eagerly, he sought to let others know about the persecution of Christians in Russia and about the courage of those who stand ready to die for their faith. He spoke often of how the spirit is stronger than the flesh; how under the most dreadful conditions the spirits of many Christians were uplifted. Like a modern apostle, Sergei spoke with the conviction born of experience about Jesus, his Lord, Who had the power to heal, deliver, forgive and redeem.

As I met with Sergei, he told me how he had traveled many miles preaching in colleges and churches through-out Canada and the United States. Still, what was most unusual about this young Russian was his sense of mission and purpose. He spoke as though he had an impending awareness that time was running out.

He confided to me that his life had been threatened by Russian nationalists both while he was in Canada and the United States, and that he sensed he would die at the hands of the Russians in such a way that it would look like suicide. Russia was angry that one of her special sons had defected. Her anger against Sergei was so strong that his life would be the price he would pay, not only for his defection, but also for publishing the truth about Russian persecution of Christians.

Sergei told me that he would rather die a free man than live in Russia in bondage. He was willing to die a martyr's death for the very cause that he was once so outraged against. He had come to understand the perfect love of the young girl who was the catalyst for his conversion to Christ. He had received that same gift of agape love which conquers all, even death itself. Finally, he had learned that the true purpose of life lies in Jesus Christ alone.

Three months after my meeting with Sergei, he was shot and killed in a hotel room at a ski resort in southern California. As he had predicted, a cloud of mystery surrounded his death. The coroner ruled the death a suicide and newspapers carried the story from coast to coast. Later, the suicide decision was changed to one of "accidental death."

Sergei's body was sent to Washington D.C., where it was laid to rest in the Russian section of Arlington National Cemetery. Though his life was short-lived, he did experience the fullness of a life-giving relationship with Jesus Christ. He had also known, at last, the perfect love from God's throne that encourages one to cherish Christ above all things—even life itself.

EPILOGUE

OUR LOVE

In this book, we have seen that *agape love* is essential if we are to love one another as Christ has commanded us. We already know from experience that all too often we cannot love as we should, or as we would like to, because it is not within our human capacity to do so. It is only when we are able to honestly acknowledge our inability to love and when we are willing to ask for God's agape love to flow through us that we can receive the power to truly love those around us.

According to the Scriptures, the greatest love involves supreme personal sacrifice. "Greater love hath no man than this, that a man lay down his life for his friends."

Are we willing to die for those we love? Examining ourselves honestly, the answer would most frequently be "no." Such an answer immediately reveals the big difference between God's love and our love. Remember, God's agape love carries with it the promise that Jesus has already fulfilled on the cross, *"I love you enough that I would die for you."*

Do we really need reminders of the limitations of our human loving? Unfortunately, the answer is "yes" because we tend to forget our need for God's love. So that we might understand the difference between God's love and our own, I have divided human love into some of its basic components. I realize, of course, that there are exceptions, and that the examples from the illustrations that follow are not the last word on the subject. They merely help to substantiate the temporary and conditional nature of human love, and how often it is merely a "taking."

The following expressions of love are what I call "human ways of loving."

"I love you because you love me."
This has what I call *conditional love* at its roots. The love that is given is done so merely because love is presently received in return.

"I love you because I want you to love me."
This is *barter love*. Such a love is based upon the prospect that if I love a person now, that very person might love me in the future.

"I love you now because you once showed love to me."
This is *law of return love*. Such love is given for love received in the past.

"I love you because you are attractive."
We all recognize this as *physical love*. Here human love is given on the basis of the physical characteristics in a person.

"I love you because you agree with me."
This is *social love*. Love is given on the basis of the conformity of the loved one to the philosophy of the lover.

"I love you because it's the religious thing to do."
This is what I call *moral obligation love*. This is a common kind of love among Christian people. It is a kind

of non-love that masquerades behind the attitude, "I can't stomach you, but I accept you, or tolerate you, because my religion says I have to."

Frightening as though it may seem, as we begin to reexamine our relationships, we find that our human love is wanting. We can clearly see that human love is often defined by a manner of taking from the loved one. God's agape love, on the other hand, is a giving; "for God so loved the world, that he *gave* . . ." And the only true way for us to give to another, without expecting something in return, is for each of us to ask for God's agape love to fill our hearts.

If agape love could be defined as were the different ways of human love, I believe it would be like this:

"I love you (I really experience a giving, selfless love) because God has placed within me His wonderful love for you."

Surprisingly, we find in Scripture that the first person who prayed that God's love would be placed in the hearts of His children was Jesus. In the Gospel of John, chapter sixteen, Jesus prayed, "Father, I will that they also, whom thou hast given me, be with me where I am; that they may behold my glory, which thou hast given me: for thou lovedst me before the foundation of the world . . . And I have declared unto them thy name, and will declare it; *that the love wherewith thou hast loved me may be in them,* and I in them."

There is, then, no real love outside of Christ. Apart from Him there is only emotional feeling and infatuation which is unreliable and subject to change. Indeed, Scripture tells us that apart from God we can do nothing, and that certainly includes loving one another.

The stories in this book have born witness to the fact that many have tried to love in their own strength and have failed. It was only when they were willing to surrender their failures and their lives to Jesus and let His divine love flow through them that they were able to truly love—and, in loving, to be victorious.

The world needs love. More now than ever before, it needs the love of God—*agape* love—shed abroad in our hearts by the Holy Spirit. And, it desperately needs to see that love expressed first in the lives of the people who preach about it the most, the Christians.

We who bear His name need to pray for a special anointing of His agape love, for it is only in so doing that we shall ever be able to love in deed and in truth as He has commanded us.

ADDENDUM

LOVE'S SOURCE

AGAPE LOVE IN THE SCRIPTURES

With the many Scriptures *on* love in the New Testament and the instructions *to* love that the early church received, we can see how very important love is in the life of a believer in Jesus Christ.

The most complete description or definition of agape love is found, of course, in the Bible. And first Corinthians, chapter thirteen, contains the clearest picture of the many facets of agape love. It is interesting to note that, much to the contrary of the impression of love given by our American culture, there are no references in first Corinthians thirteen to the "overwhelming feelings" that are the main emphasis of human love. Rather, agape love is born of the action of receiving that love from God and then allowing it to flow from us to others.

Let's look at the Holy Spirit's definition of God's love:

"Love is patient, love is kind, and is not jealous; love does not brag and is not arrogant, does not act unbecomingly; it does not seek its own, is not provoked, does not take into account a wrong suffered, does not rejoice in unrighteousness, but rejoices with the truth; bears all things, believes all things, hopes all things, endures all things. Love never fails" (Corinthians 13:4-8 NASB).

The love that God requires of us can be overwhelming, yet, it simply reaffirms the impossibility of having it on our own. Trying to live up to that Scripture without the Lord's help is the cause of many Christians' failure to successfully obey His commandment to love.

But, we can thank God we have the assurance even in the sin of not loving that, "If we confess our sins, he is faithful and just to forgive us our sins, and to cleanse us from all unrighteousness (1 John 1:9).

And, we can further thank Him that by asking the Lord to give us His agape love, to place the love described in first Corinthians thirteen in our hearts by the power of the Holy Spirit, we can be victorious! It is a blessing to remember that God doesn't expect anything *from* us that He hasn't given *to* us already.

The following Scripture sections are a study on agape love. So that you might understand the utmost significance of having this love, I will begin with the Source, God, and move on to the all-encompassing emphasis on love in the Kingdom of God.

I trust that these Scriptures will be fruitful and increase each believer's understanding of *the higher love*.

GOD'S LOVE FOR MAN

As God the Father is the Source of all things, He is also the originator of agape love. As you can see below, we have confidence in knowing that He loved us first, both before we received Jesus as Lord and Savior, and afterwards as His children.

For God so loved the world, that he gave his only begotten Son, that whosoever believeth in him should not perish, but have everlasting life (John 3:16).

Jesus answered and said unto him, If a man love me, he will keep my words: and *my Father will love him*, and we will come unto him, and make our abode with him (John 14:23).

For the Father himself loveth you, because ye have loved me, and have believed that I came from God (John 16:27).

And that the world may know that *thou* [the Father] hast sent me, and *hast loved them, as thou hast loved me* [Jesus] (John 17:23).

Because *the love of God* is shed abroad in our hearts by the Holy Ghost which is given unto us (Romans 5:5).

But *God commendeth his love toward us*, in that, while we were yet sinners, Christ died for us (Romans 5:8).

Nay, in all these things we are more than conquerors *through him that loved us*. For I am persuaded, that neither death, nor life, nor angels, nor principalities, nor powers, nor things present, nor things to come, Nor height, nor depth, nor any other creature, shall be able to separate us from *the love of God*, which is in Christ Jesus our Lord (Romans 8:37-39).

Every man according as he purposeth in his heart, so let him give; not grudgingly, or of necessity: *for God loveth a cheerful giver* (2 Corinthians 9:7).

The grace of the Lord Jesus Christ, and *the love of God*, and the communion of the Holy Ghost, be with you all (2 Corinthians 13:14).

But after that the kindness and *love of God* our Savior *toward man* appeared (Titus 3:4).

For whom the Lord loveth he chasteneth, and scourgeth every son whom he receiveth (Hebrews 12:6).

But whoso keepeth his word, in Him verily is *the love of God perfected* (1 John 2:5).

Behold, *what manner of love the Father hath bestowed upon us*, that we should be called the sons of God (1 John 3:1).

Hereby perceive we *the love of God*, because he laid down his life for us (1 John 3:16).

Beloved, let us love one another: *for love is of God*; and every one that loveth is born of God, and knoweth God. He that loveth not, knoweth not God; for *God is love*. In this was manifested *the love of God toward us*, because that God sent his only begotten Son into the world, that we might live through him (1 John 4:7-9).

Herein is love, not that we loved God, *but that he loved us*, and sent his Son to be the propitiation for our sins (1 John 4:10).

And we have known and believed *the love that God hath to us. God is love;* and he that dwelleth in love dwelleth in God, and God in him (1 John 4:16).

We love him, because *he first loved us* (1 John 4:19).

CHRIST'S LOVE FOR MAN

Agape love is made clearer and more personal to the individual through Jesus Christ. Scripture had much to say to us about the love of Christ for us.

Now before the feast of the passover, when Jesus knew that his hour was come that he should depart out of this world unto the Father, *having loved his own which were in the world, he loved them unto the end* (John 13:1).

A new commandment I give unto you, That ye love one another; *as I have loved you*, that ye love also one another (John 13:34).

And he that loveth me shall be loved of my Father, and *I will love him*, and will manifest myself to him (John 14:21).

As the Father hath loved me, *so have I loved you* (John 15:9).

This is my commandment, That ye love one another, *as I have loved you. Greater love hath no man than this*, that a man lay down his life for his friends (John 15:12,13).

Who shall separate us from *the love of Christ*? (Romans 8:35).

For *the love of Christ* constraineth [controls] us (2 Corinthians 5:14).

I am crucified with Christ: nevertheless I live; yet not I, but Christ liveth in me: and the life which I now live in the flesh I live by the faith of the Son of God, *who loved me, and gave himself up for me* (Galatians 2:20).

That ye, being rooted and grounded in love, May ye be able to comprehend with all saints what is *the breadth*, and *length*, and *depth*, and *height*; And *to know the love of Christ*, which passeth knowledge (Ephesians 3:17-19).

And walk in love, *as Christ also hath loved us*, and hath given himself for us . . . (Ephesians 5:2)

Husbands, love your wives, *even as Christ also loved the church*, and gave himself for it (Ephesians 5:25).

And the grace of our Lord was exceeding abundant with faith *and love which is in Christ Jesus* (1 Timothy 1:14).

Hold fast the form of sound words, which thou hast heard of me, in faith *and love which is in Christ Jesus* (2 Timothy 1:13).

And from Jesus Christ, who is the faithful witness, and

the first-begotten of the dead, and the prince of the kings of the earth. Unto *him that loved us*, and washed us from our sins in his own blood (Revelation 1:5).

Behold, I [Jesus] will make them to come and worship before thy feet and *to know that I have loved thee* (Revelations 3:9).

COMMANDMENTS TO LOVE

Jesus gave a new commandment to his disciples, and to all of us that follow after him, that we should love our friends and our enemies, not just in any way that we choose, but even as he loved us, being willing to die for us. And, Jesus' statements are seldom suggestions, but rather commandments to be obeyed.

But I say unto you, *Love your enemies*, bless them that curse you, do good to them that hate you, and pray for them which despitefully use you, and persecute you (Matthew 5:44)

And the second [great commandment] is like unto it, *Thou shalt love thy neighbor as thyself* (Matthew 22:39).

And the second is like, namely this, *Thou shalt love thy neighbor as theyself* (Mark 12:31).

165

But I say unto you which hear, *Love your enemies*, do good to them which hate you . . . For if ye love them which love you, what then have ye? For sinners also love those who love them . . . *But love ye your enemies* (Luke 6:27, 32, 35).

A new commandment I give unto you, That *ye love one another*, as I have loved you, that *ye also love one another*. By this shall all men know that ye are my disciples, if *ye have love one to another* (John 13:34, 35).

As the Father hath loved me, so have I loved you: *continue ye in my love*. If ye keep my commandments, ye shall abide in my love; even as I have kept my Father's commandments, and abide in his love (John 15:9, 10).

This is my commandment, that *ye love one another*, as I have loved you (John 15:12).

These things I command you, that *ye love one another* (John 15:17).

MAN'S LOVE FOR GOD

As God, the Father, and God, the Son, loved us, so also are we to love them. With the command to love, comes the way to do it (by obedience), plus some of the rewards in loving God.

COMMANDS

Jesus said unto him, *Thou shalt love the Lord thy God* with all thy heart, and with all thy soul, and with all thy mind. This is the first and great commandment (Matthew 22:37,38).

And he answering said, *Thou shalt love the Lord thy God* with all thy heart, and with all thy soul, and with all thy strength, and with all thy mind (Luke 10:27).

Jesus said unto them, If God were your Father, *ye would love me* (John 8:42).

If ye love me, keep my commandments (John 14:15).

He that hath my commandments, and keepeth them, *he it is that loveth me* (John 14:21).

Jesus answered and said unto him, *If a man love me*, he will keep my words (John 14:23).

167

If a man say, I love God, and hateth his brother, he is a liar: for he that loveth not his brother whom he hath seen, how can he love God whom he hath not seen? And this commandment have we from him, That *he who loveth God* love his brother also (1 John 4:20, 21).

By this we know we love the children of God, *when we love God*, and keep his commandments. For *this is the love of God*, that we keep his commandments (1 John 5:2, 3).

And this is love, that we walk after his commandments (2 John 6).

REWARDS

And we know that all things work together for good *to them that love God*, to them who are the called according to his purpose (Romans 8:28).

But as it is written, Eye hath not seen, nor ear heard, neither have entered into the heart of man, the things which God hath prepared *for them that love him* (1 Corinthians 2:9).

Grace be with them all them *that love our Lord Jesus Christ* in sincerity (Ephesians 6:24)

Blessed is the man that endureth temptation: for when he is tried, he shall receive the crown of life, which the Lord hath promised to them *that love him* (James 1:12).

Hearken, my beloved brethren. Hath God not chosen the poor of this world rich in faith, and heirs of the kingdom which he hath promised *to them that love him*? (James 2:5).

LOVE ONE ANOTHER

The most frequent admonition given by the apostles of the early church is: love one another. *The importance of obeying this commandment to love the brethren with agape love is stated over and over again. Here are a few of those scriptures.*

Owe no man any thing, but to *love one another*: for he that loveth another hath fulfilled the law (Romans 13:8).

Seeing ye have purified your souls in obeying the truth through the Spirit unto *unfeigned love of the brethren*, see that ye *love one another* with a pure heart fervently (1 Peter 1:22).

He that *loveth his brother* abideth in the light, and there is no occasion of stumbling in him (1 John 2:10).

For this is the message that ye heard from the beginning, that we should *love one another* (1 John 3:11).

We know that we have passed from death unto life, because we *love the brethren* (1 John 3:14).

Hereby perceive we the love of God, because he laid down his life for us: and *we ought to lay down our lives for the brethren* (1 John 3:16).

And this is his commandment, That we should believe on the name of his Son Jesus Christ, and *love one another*, as he gave us commandment (1 John 3:23).

Beloved, let us love one another: for love is of God; and every one that loveth is born of God, and knoweth God. He that loveth not, knoweth not God; for God is love (1 John 4:7,8).

Herein is love, not that we loved God, but that he loved us, and sent his Son to be the propitiation for our sins. Beloved, if God so loved us, *we ought also to love one another*. No man hath seen God at any time. *If we love one another*, God dwelleth in us, and his love is perfected in us (1 John 4:10-12).

And this commandment have we from him, That he who loveth God *love his brother also* (1 John 4:21).

And now I beseech thee, lady, not as though I wrote a new commandment unto thee, but that which we had from the beginning, that we *love one another* (2 John 5).

LOVE IN THE KINGDOM OF GOD

Finally, agape love is found to be the greatest influence in the Kingdom of God, directing all of our steps and an integral part of all of our actions. There is nothing as far reaching or all-encompassing as agape love.

For in Jesus Christ neither circumcision availeth any thing, nor uncircumcision; but *faith which worketh by love* (Galatians 5:6).

For, brethren, ye have been called unto liberty; only use not liberty for an occasion to the flesh, but *by love serve one another* (Galatians 5:13).

That Christ may dwell in your hearts by faith; that ye, *being rooted and grounded in love*, May be able *to comprehend* with all saints what is *the breadth, and length, and depth, and height; And to know the love of Christ,* which passeth knowledge, that ye might be filled with all the fulness of God (Ephesians 3:17-19).

I therefore, the prisoner of the Lord, beseech you that ye walk worthy of the vocation wherewith ye are called, With all lowliness and meekness, with long-suffering, *forbearing one another in love*; Endeavoring to keep the unity of the Spirit in the bond of peace (Ephesians 4:1-3).

But *speaking the truth in love*, [the Church] may grow up into him in all things, which is the head, even Christ (Ephesians 4:15).

From whom the whole body fitly joined together and compacted by that which every joint supplieth, according to the effectual working in the measure of every part, *maketh increase of the body unto the edifying of itself in love* (Ephesians 4:16).

Be ye therefore followers of God, as dear children; *And walk in love*, as Christ also hath loved us, and hath given himself for us an offering and a sacrifice to God for a sweet-smelling savor (Ephesians 5:1-2).

Husbands *love your wives*, even as Christ also loved the church, and gave himself for it . . . So ought men to *love their wives* as their own bodies. *He that loveth his wife loveth himself* (Ephesians 5:25,28).

Peace be to the brethren, and *love with faith*, from God the Father and the Lord Jesus Christ. Grace be with all them that *love* our Lord Jesus Christ *in sincerity* (Ephesians 6:23).

If there be therefore any consolation in Christ, if any *comfort of love*, if any fellowship of the Spirit . . . Fulfill ye my joy, that ye be likeminded, *having the same love,* being of one accord, of one mind (Philippians 2:1,2).

Who also declared unto us your *love in the Spirit* (Colossians 1:8).

That their hearts might be comforted, *being knit together in love* (Colossians 2:2).

Remembering without ceasing your work of faith, and *labor of love*, and patience of hope in our Lord Jesus Christ (1 Thessalonians 1:3).

And the Lord make you to *increase and abound in love one toward another*, and toward all men, even as we do toward you: To the end he may stablish your hearts unblameable in holiness before God (1 Thessalonians 3:12,13).

Let us hold fast the profession of our faith without wavering; for he is faithful that promised; And let us consider one another to *provoke unto love* and to good works (Hebrews 10:23,24).

Honor all men. *Love the brotherhood.* Fear God. Honor the king. (1 Peter 2:17).

Finally, be ye all one mind, having compassion one of another; *love as brethren*, be pitiful, be courteous (1 Peter 3:8).

And above all things have fervent charity [love] among yourselves: for charity [*love*] *shall cover the multitude of sins* (1 Peter 4:8).

But whoso keepeth his word, in him verily is *the love of God perfected:* hereby know we that we are in him (1 John 2:5).

Love not the world, neither the things that are in the world. If any man love the world, the love of the Father is not in him (1 John 2:15).

My little children, *let us not love in word, neither in tongue; but in deed and in truth* (1 John 3:18).

There is *no fear in love*; but *perfect love casteth out fear:* because fear hath torment. He that feareth is not made perfect in love (1 John 4:18).

But ye, beloved, building up yourselves on your most holy faith, praying in the Holy Ghost, *Keep yourselves in the love of God*, looking for the mercy of our Lord Jesus Christ unto eternal life (Jude 20,21).